# HURRICANE SANDY
# ON NEW JERSEY'S
# FORGOTTEN SHORE

# HURRICANE SANDY ON NEW JERSEY'S FORGOTTEN SHORE

Abigail Perkiss

CORNELL UNIVERSITY PRESS  ITHACA AND LONDON

First published 2022 by Cornell University Press

Library of Congress Cataloging-in-Publication Data
Names: Perkiss, Abigail, 1981– author.
Title: Hurricane Sandy on New Jersey's forgotten shore / Abigail Perkiss.
Description: Ithaca [New York] : Cornell University Press, 2022. | Includes
    bibliographical references and index.
Identifiers: LCCN 2021062615 (print) | LCCN 2021062616 (ebook) |
    ISBN 9781501709852 (hardcover) | ISBN 9781501709869 (paperback) |
    ISBN 9781501764325 (pdf) | ISBN 9781501764332 (epub)
Subjects: LCSH: Hurricane Sandy, 2012—Social aspects. | Hurricanes—Social
    aspects—New Jersey. | New Jersey—Social conditions—21st century.
Classification: LCC QC945 .P475 2022 (print) | LCC QC945 (ebook) |
    DDC 363.34/92209749—dc23/eng20220314
LC record available at https://lccn.loc.gov/2021062615
LC ebook record available at https://lccn.loc.gov/2021062616

# Contents

On October 29, 2012, a devastating storm pummeled the eastern coastline of North America. Rain and wind bore down for two days. When the water receded, 233 people were dead from the Caribbean to Canada, 43 of them in New Jersey.[1] More than 8.5 million households across twenty-one states were without power at the height of the outages. In New Jersey, 62 percent of customers suffered blackouts.[2] Hurricane Sandy compromised 346,000 primary residences in the Garden State; 55,000 of those homes were either destroyed or incurred substantial damage.[3] The worst flooding occurred in Staten Island, New York, and throughout the four New Jersey counties along the coast. "In Monmouth and Ocean Counties," a Department of Environmental Protection assessment report indicated, "post-storm surveys confirmed entire communities were flooded, with houses washed off foundations and cars and boats carried well inland by the surge."[4] Across those counties, in particular, the loss was staggering.

New Jersey has long been a bellwether of US environmental trends. With the highest population density in the nation, the state ranks second in the United States, behind only Florida, for the most homes susceptible to chronic flooding because of rising sea levels.[5] By 2045, more than 62,000 residential properties will be at risk across the state. By century's end, that number is projected to reach 250,000.[6] These statistics do not take into account additional growth, in terms of new home development, public buildings, military bases, or additional transportation infrastructure. This compounded impact could be devastating for the state's economy; forecasting further ahead, it will likely be devastating for the nation as well.[7] As geographer James Mitchell wrote, "Wherever the world's developed areas are going with respect to natural disasters, New Jersey will get there first."[8]

With the increasing ferocity of storms across the globe, longstanding political debates over the nature of climate change, and the ongoing need to manage the impact of environmental conditions on the built environment, the relationship between human action and natural hazards has become one of the most pressing issues of our time. But as these birds-eye political debates and policy decisions capture headlines, individual voices often get lost. This book recovers those voices.[9] Drawing on nearly seventy oral history interviews conducted in the three years following Hurricane Sandy, it documents the uneven recovery of the storm along the Bayshore: the 115 square miles of coastline running from Sandy Hook at the lip of the Atlantic Ocean to South Amboy at the mouth of the Raritan River—New Jersey's forgotten shore.[10]

The experiences of Sandy for those who make their lives on the Bayshore offers insight into how we prepare for, survive, and respond to disaster. These experiences at once reveal the human toll of disaster and the human capacity for resilience. Collette Kennedy, who moved to Keyport just weeks before Sandy hit, was so looking forward to celebrating her first Halloween in her new home. Linda Gonzalez penned poems by candlelight as rain and wind beat down on her beloved Union Beach, knowing that those might be the last moments of relative calm that she would experience for months. James Butler erected a washed-up plastic Christmas tree at the corner of Jersey Avenue and Shore Road and became a national icon representing "Jersey Strong." And Mary Jane and Roger Michalak, married forty-seven years, realized that they wouldn't be able to raise themselves through a hole in their attic and instead sat down on their bed together, waiting for the water to wash over them. These voices, individually and collectively, offer a portrait of a devastating storm and of the network of relationships as victims, volunteers, and state and federal agencies came together afterward to rebuild.

Their stories shed light on the short-term preparedness initiatives that municipal and state governments undertook, which successfully mitigated the risk to human life, and the long-term planning decisions that created the conditions for catastrophic property damage. They honor the role of local and national media outlets in galvanizing recovery efforts, and they call out the feelings of marginalization for those residents whose communities the television cameras ignored. They illuminate the ways in which Hurricane Sandy remade the role of social media in disaster preparedness and recovery, at a time when long-term power outages and cellular disruptions transformed Facebook into the most reliable mode of communication. They amplify the challenges of accommodation in disaster preparedness, and the particular challenges that post-storm flood-insurance regulations posed for those who simply could not walk up extra stairs to their front door. And they lay bare the ways that climate change and sea-level rise are creating critical vulnerabilities in the most densely populated areas in the nation.

This book is not a comprehensive evaluation of Hurricane Sandy in New Jersey. It is not a blueprint of postdisaster response or a polemical treatise on what went wrong. Instead, it offers an intimate window into the human impact of a devastating storm and the intended and unintended consequences of long-term policy decisions that created the conditions for such destruction. It is the story of the individual choices that residents made in the days preceding landfall and the personal dilemmas they faced as they struggled to rebuild their lives. Out of these individual stories emerges the story of the Bayshore itself—the land, the waterways, the homes, businesses, and community spaces, and the people who inhabit them.[11]

# Acknowledgments

In December 2012, I was sitting in my office at Kean University, when my cell phone rang. It was Kate Scott, one of my closest friends from graduate school, then the assistant historian at the US Senate Historical Office. It was rare to receive phone calls from friends during the workday, rarer still for them to come from Capitol Hill. I picked up.

When I walked into my department chair's office ten minutes later and concocted a plan to work with students in an advanced undergraduate oral history seminar the following spring to document the aftermath of Hurricane Sandy, I had no way of anticipating the ten-year odyssey I was about to embark on, the culmination of which is the publication of this book. Nor could I have imagined the outpouring of support I received at every step of this project.

I am deeply indebted to Linda Shopes, Stephen Sloan, and D'Ann Penner for sitting down with this relatively green oral historian and helping me work through what it would mean to go down the path of disaster testimonies, as well as highlighting the potential pitfalls that might befall me and my students along the way. As Stephen told me in January 2013, weeks before I walked into the classroom for our first meeting, "I was warned away from doing this work [on Hurricane Katrina] back in 2005. I'm glad I didn't listen."

My thanks, as well, to David Caruso, Janneken Smucker, Kathy Nasstrom, Troy Reeves, Doug Boyd, Annie Valk, and the multitude of other colleagues turned friends at Oral History in the Mid-Atlantic Region and the Oral History Association. When I started this work, I was still looking for a professional home that pulled together my various and diverse scholarly and pedagogical interests and welcomed my ideas. I found it in these organizations.

I extend my gratitude to Carly Goodman, Matt Johnson, Monica Mercado, Sharon Musher, and Mary Rizzo, with whom I spent my sabbatical, writing chapters, sipping coffee, sharing critiques, and trading sympathies. To Audra Wolfe, for encouraging me to think bigger when I was first pitching the project as a book. To Kate Scott, for her early and ongoing commitment to this work, and for her regular check-ins and good cheer. To Caren Brenman, who told me that it was okay to hit pause when the words weren't coming—for a little while, at least. To Monica Hesse, fellow member of the Bryn Mawr College class of '03, whose writing offered inspiration when I struggled to find my voice. To Jeff Barg, who read the full book while relaxing in the Maine woods, and to Collette Kennedy, who read a subsequent draft in an Atlantic City hotel room. And to Dan Royles, who not only read substantial sections of this book but also texted me one summer day in 2014, when I was nursing my three-month-old daughter, and asked if I wanted to collaborate on a digital humanities initiative to bring our Staring Out to Sea interviews to a wider audience. Had we known then where that partnership would take us. . .

Portions of the backmatter of this book, chronicling the development of Staring Out to Sea, were previously published in "Staring Out to Sea and the Transformative Power of Oral History for Undergraduate Interviewers," *Oral History Review* 43, no. 2 (September 2016): 392–407.

Thank you to my colleagues in the Kean history department—I count myself lucky to share my days with you. To David Farber, Beth Bailey, Richard Immerman, and Laura Levitt, for your continued support and encouragement. To Kean University, Stockton University, the Tuckerton Seaport and Baymen's Museum, Oral History in the Mid-Atlantic Region, the Oral History Association, the New Jersey Council for the Humanities, and the New Jersey Historical Commission, for investing in this work, and to Joe Cronin, Lindy Foreman, and Susan Gannon, for your assistance in pursuing that support. To Doug Boyd (again) and the staff at the Louie B. Nunn Center for Oral History at the University of Kentucky, where all of the Staring Out to Sea interviews are now stored. To the external reviewers and the editorial and faculty boards at Cornell University Press, for their encouragement and feedback on this book. To Michael McGandy and the editorial team at Cornell University Press; I am grateful for the relationship we've built over twelve years and two books. And to Clare Jones and the production team, who helped guide this project to completion.

Thank you to Alicia Hill, Trudi-Ann Lawrence, Brittany Le Strange, Mary Piasecki, Abdelfatth Rasheed, and Arij Syed, the original Staring Out to Sea team, who showed up to class in January 2013 with only a passing sense of what the next sixteen weeks would hold, and who worked to create something far better than the sum of its individual parts. Here's to the hours we spent together staring at maps of New Jersey, defining the terms of the project, recruiting narrators, trying on titles, and camping out at hotel breakfast bars from Washington, DC, to Oklahoma City, crafting analyses of what it all meant. Your trust gave me the confidence to think big.

Thank you to Jennifer Block-Lerner, Lindsay Liotta, and Christina Cooke, for helping to prepare these students for the interview experience; Jennifer Block-Lerner also continued down this path with me in our exploration of trauma-sensitive oral history. To Ruqayyah Abdullah and Christina Leedy, who joined the interview team in subsequent phases of the project and dove in with excitement and respect in equal measures. To the students in Dan Royles's digital humanities course at Stockton University, especially Chelsea Mendoza, for indexing the interviews and developing the prototype digital library. To Ian Fahey, Gabe De Luca, Matthew Rela, Alexander Mirabal, and Eric Rosa in the Kean Computer Science program, as well as their faculty adviser Patricia Morreale, for their work on building out the original website for the project.

To my family and friends, thank you for the time in the woods, the happy hours and coffee dates that more recently turned to Zoom chats and masked walks, the deep dives into politics and the suggestions of Netflix escapism, the Little Adventures, and for being part of our ever-expanding community in Philadelphia and around the world. Thank you, too, for your reassurances that I am the person to write this book, for your patience when I wasn't able to write, and for your supportive pushes to get me started again. To my dad, equal parts cheerleader, babysitter, and confidante. To my mom, for showing me the value in the long game—finishing her PhD at the age of sixty-four—and for becoming an unlikely writing buddy. To my sister, for her quiet but persistent support and for taking such good care of the pups. To Brent, my favorite adventurer in crime. To Zoe, who joined us in utero on several Staring Out to Sea interviews and presentations; who reminds me daily of the value in good playgrounds, impromptu sing-a-longs, drippy ice cream cones, creek adventures, and lazy weekend mornings; and who asked me almost every evening during the summer of 2018, "Mama, did you write today?" And to Simon, whose early months of life may have made writing a challenge, but whose easy smiles, big belly laughs, and endless curiosity made the missed deadlines worth it.

And finally, to all of the narrators of the Staring Out to Sea Oral History Project. Thank you for inviting us into your lives and trusting us to do justice with your stories.

# FRANKENSTORM

When Collette Kennedy moved into her new home in Keyport, New Jersey, in mid-October 2012, she was elated. The modest ranch with cornflower blue siding; the attached garage, gleaming white; the small front yard, just a mile off the water—it was perfect. She had spent the past ten years walking the beaches of Keyport and the adjacent Union Beach. On three separate occasions, she had put bids on real estate in the area, but the sales kept falling through. Now she was finally home, in her "happy place."[1]

Halloween was coming. On October 14, she bought hay and pumpkins to decorate her new yard. It was the first time that she had her own house for trick-or-treating, and she decided to splurge. The following Sunday, the twentieth, she spent the morning setting up displays, hanging spider webs, and repositioning hay bales until everything was just right.[2] On Monday, the National Hurricane Center announced that the ball of energy forming in the western Caribbean now had a name. "Tropical Storm Sandy," wrote Gary Szatkowski, chief meteorologist at the National Weather Service office in Mount Holly, New Jersey, on Tuesday morning, "is expected to reach hurricane strength on Wednesday. It will continue northward. This storm will bring multiple potential threats to the [mid-Atlantic] region. . . . The takeaway is that our region could come close to the path of a very dangerous storm. Our region is clearly at risk."[3] By noon, the report had gone out to weather bureaus serving more than twelve million people across four states. The next day, Collette Kennedy took down her decorations and stowed them in her garage.[4]

In the days before Hurricane Sandy collided with the Eastern Seaboard, forecasters and meteorologists worked to predict the storm's track, to warn residents of its potential for destruction, and to compel government officials to take appropriate actions. And indeed, administrators responded. As the storm hurtled toward the mid-Atlantic, local, state, and federal agencies implemented emergency-management protocols, sent out widespread notices to their communities, and issued evacuation warnings along New Jersey's 210 miles of coastline.[5]

Over the previous half-century, New Jersey officials had focused on creating effective systems for protecting human life in the face of increasingly devastating storms along the coastline. And with coordinated evacuation routes, advances in communication, and sophisticated emergency-response protocols, officials had reduced the risk of injury and loss of life. But this emphasis on human peril obscured the weaknesses in infrastructure that came with increased physical development and growing population density along the coast.[6] Sandy was "a departure from all known meteorological history," as the physicist Adam Sobel wrote, and a week of steadfast preparation wasn't enough to ready the shoreline for what was to come.[7] Longstanding practices in land management and coastal development created critical vulnerabilities in areas that had been specifically designated as high risk. Sandy unmasked these vulnerabilities—with devastating results.

Sandy developed as a tropical storm over the western Caribbean Sea on October 22. As it marched steadily north, its intensity grew. When it hit Kingston, Jamaica, on October 24, it was a Category 1 hurricane. By the time it moved back out to sea, one person was dead, and officials estimated that it had done close to $100 million in damage. Close to two thousand people were sleeping in shelters, and 70 percent of residents across the island were without power.[8] When Sandy landed in Cuba the next day, the storm had reached Category 3 status. There, it took the lives of eleven people and destroyed fifteen thousand homes.[9] Its strength ebbed and flowed as it swirled through the Caribbean, downgrading to a tropical depression and then surging back to a Category 1 hurricane. By the time Sandy made its way up the Atlantic coast of the United States, it was, wrote the journalist Kathryn Miles, "the largest storm the planet had ever seen—a storm big enough to consume the entire Eastern Seaboard and beyond."[10]

The National Weather Service predicted that Sandy would join together with two cold fronts as it made its way up the coast, turning it, wrote one *Wall Street Journal* reporter, into a "post-tropical cyclone, or nor'easter, unleashing record low-pressure readings and wind gusts to seventy miles an hour as far inland as western Pennsylvania and western New York."[11] As the journalists Amy Ellis Nutt and Stephen Stirling of the *Star Ledger* wrote, "The mammoth storm is part hurricane, part nor'easter, and is expected to pummel Americans from south of Maryland to Maine and drench some areas with at least a foot of rain, others with two feet of snow, and homes and businesses along 800 miles with forty to fifty mph winds."[12] On Thursday, October 25, with a nod toward Halloween the following week, Jim Cisco of the National Oceanic and Atmospheric Administration (NOAA) coined the term "Frankenstorm." The winds from Sandy, he wrote, would be "incorporated into a hybrid vortex over the mid-Atlantic and Northeast next Tuesday. . . . [The] unusual merger" was expected to "settle back toward the interior Northeast through Halloween, inviting perhaps a ghoulish nickname for the cyclone along the lines of 'Frankenstorm,' an allusion to Mary Shelley's Gothic creature of synthesized elements."[13] By that point, forecasters were grasping—for what to call the storm and for how to put it the context of past precedent. The scope and historic trajectory of Sandy confounded them.

And that was precisely the problem. Sandy was not just a hurricane. In the storm's weeklong tear through the Caribbean and Atlantic, it had reinvented itself in so many different iterations and crossed paths with so many pressure systems, tidal shifts, and tropical surges that forecasters around the world were struggling to keep up. "We want to name it," CNN meteorologist Rob Marciano explained, "because it's unlike anything we've seen meteorologically. At first, when nicknames were thrown out there, the meteorologists were having fun with it—it was interesting to us, and no one believed, frankly, that the models would continue this trend."[14] But they did. And by week's end, meteorologists had stopped joking.

Along New Jersey's Bayshore, the 115 square miles of coastline along the Sandy Hook and Raritan Bays, residents struggled to keep pace with the changing storm predictions. Linda Gonzalez, sitting in the Union Beach home that she shared with her husband and their children and grandchildren, spent the days before landfall fixated on the Weather Channel. Each morning, she turned on the television, eager for an update, wondering whether the storm would hit, how strong it would grow, and where the worst damage would be. As a lifelong resident of New Jersey, she had lived through hurricanes before. But her gut told her that this one would be different. The surges. The full moon. The low pressure. She knew something big was coming.[15]

Early in the week, she went to the grocery store for extra batteries, canned food, and bottled water. "Just in case," she said, "because you always have to have that 'just in case' supply." At first, she prepared for a week without power. Then news reports began predicting as many as three weeks. She went back to the store and filled her cart with toilet paper, paper towels, more bottled water. The lines were growing by then—she needed to make the trip count. She stocked her freezer with food, forgetting that everything would spoil in a prolonged power outage. She loaded her pantry with chips and cereal, "anything you could eat without . . . having to cook." She thought she was ready for whatever Sandy might bring.[16]

Four miles to the east, William (Bill) and Henry (Hank) Gelhaus, co-owners of the Keansburg Amusement Park, spent the days before the storm dismantling the rides and attractions at the park. They took down Pharaoh's Fury and stowed the bumper cars in their large garage. They secured the Spookhouse, which had opened in 1931 as one of the world's first dark rides (indoor amusement park experiences that carry passengers through scenes characterized by dim lighting and animated effects), and pulled the Jolly Caterpillar, the very first ride on the Keansburg Boardwalk. They hoped that the berm and dune system would protect them, as it had in the past. Still, the brothers didn't want to take any chances.[17]

They had lived on the coast long enough to know what happens when the system fails.[18] Their grandfather, William Gelhaus, Sr., had opened the park 108 years earlier, in 1904.[19] "He had a vision," Hank later reflected. "He knew people would want waterfront property. He filled in all that marshland and carved it into business lots."[20] Six years later, the elder Gelhaus founded the Keansburg Steamboat Company to carry New Yorkers from the city to the New Jersey Bayshore. His vision for the area bore fruit. For decades, city residents took the ferry over for a weekend escape to the Keansburg Borough, where the calm, brackish waters of the Raritan and Sandy Hook Bays come together and visitors to the asphalt boardwalk can glimpse Staten Island and Brooklyn off in the distance.[21]

Then, in 1960, Hurricane Donna wiped out the waterfront. For the next twelve years, William's son, Henry, Sr., tried to breathe life back into the boardwalk. But recovery was slow, and in 1972, he felt he had no choice but to sell the property. "He thought it was dying," Hank later recalled, ". . . [and] my brother and I were too young to take it over. . . . But let me tell you, the ink wasn't dry on the contract before he regretted it. He said it was the worst mistake of his life."[22] For twenty-three years, Hank and Bill watched as the property turned over. Then, in 1995, the owners returned to the Gelhauses. "They asked us if we wanted the park back," said Hank. "Without hesitation, we said yes. Without hesitation."[23]

By 2012, the amusement park, the oldest in the state, once again stood as a fixture on the beachfront. In the seventeen years since they had reacquired it, the brothers had invested $4 million into the site, adding a water park and thirty new rides. The facility saw an average of three hundred thousand visitors each year, and the Gelhauses had big plans for Keansburg's future; they hoped to one day turn it over to their children.[24] "My whole life is here," said Hank, who met his wife, Allison, when she came to work at the park in 1976.[25] So, when talk of another big storm began, they resolved to preserve their heritage and protect their long-term investment.

The Gelhauses' Keansburg, Gonzalez's Union Beach, and Kennedy's Keyport sit along the calm waters of the Sandy Hook Bay, three of the seventeen towns that make up the Bayshore. Though attractions like the Keansburg Amusement Park bring visitors to the area, in the early years of the twenty-first century, most people on the Bayshore were year-round residents working blue-collar jobs.[26] As of 2010, only 18 of the 2,269 housing units in Union Beach were marked for seasonal use; in Keansburg, 56 of the borough's 4,318 residences were second homes; in Port Monmouth, 13 of 1,441.[27] Located in Monmouth County just off Exit 117 of the Garden State Parkway and less than an hour from New York City, the Bayshore region is a microcosm of New Jersey: part waterfront tourism, part undeveloped natural land, part working-class rustbelt, part fierce localism.

The written history of the Bayshore dates back to the early days of European settlement, when Henry Hudson's *Halve Maen* (or *Half Moon*) made landfall along the East Coast of North America in 1609. Until that point, the New Jersey coastline was relatively undeveloped, a result of unfavorable agricultural conditions and the stronger transportation networks that the Lenni-Lenape had created along the Delaware River to the west.[28] But as Dutch and British transplants moved inland, appropriating the land and tilling the rich soil, the coastal areas encompassing Staten Island to the north and the present-day Bayshore to the south developed into strong fishing and shipping industries.[29] One of the more prominent businessmen in the area, Richard Hartshorne, purchased land from the Lenni-Lenape in 1676 to develop a fishery. Hartshorne, who had emigrated from Leicestershire, England, as early as 1669, went on to become the town clerk of Middletown and a member of the Provincial Assembly. By the time of the American Revolution, the Bayshore had become a Loyalist stronghold, with British soldiers anchored in the Sandy Hook and Raritan Bays.[30]

When the war ended, agricultural development, oyster farming, and forestry became the key economies of the region. As the region grew, stakeholders contemplated the potential risks of building so close to the water's edge. Present-day Keyport was the first section of the shoreline to be developed, because of its fertile soil, valuable old-growth timber, and modest grade rising off the water that offered relative protection from any flooding that the bay might bring in. The town's name, acquired because it was the first port to bring produce to Manhattan, bears out its reputation as a critical economic outpost. On the Kearney Plantation, which by 1811 totaled 781 acres, seventy enslaved people tilled the land, and residents traveled by boat until 1830, when three roads were laid.[31]

This new access increased the value of the land and opened the region to further development. Within five miles of the Kearneys' property were several grist mills and sawmills, processing a diverse array of crops.[32] In 1852, the Florence and Keyport Company constructed a pier in Union Beach, transforming the Bayshore into a shipping hub for northern New Jersey. With the extension of the railroad in 1890 and the construction of local train stations, enterprising real estate developers began to build new homes and subdivisions on the large tracts of farmland, and by the turn of the twentieth century, families began to move into the area, transforming it into a thriving destination community.[33]

A 1908 state ordinance reorganized the Bayshore into a series of discrete boroughs with local government structures. This institutionalized localism was further codified in 1917 with the passage of the Home Rule Act, which granted all types of local municipalities equal legal standing, regardless of size or form of governance. The legislation stated, "In construing the provisions of this subtitle, all courts shall construe the same most favorably to municipalities, it being the intention to give all municipalities to which this subtitle applies the fullest and most complete powers possible over the internal affairs of such municipalities for local self-government."[34]

For the previous century and a half, a system like this had existed informally in New Jersey, as it did in several other states, an homage to the colonial struggle against the British Crown that safeguarded the independence of individual communities against the aggregate power of the state. But as development and population growth led to the demise of the home-rule ethos around the country, in the Garden State the mandate remained strong. Whereas other states were beginning to adopt a tiered approach to governance, the 1917 New Jersey law created five distinct and equal types of municipalities in New Jersey and imbued in each the same powers of governance. Each city, borough, town, village, and township was responsible for collecting taxes, maintaining roads, running schools, and supporting such services as water, sewers, trash collection, and police and fire protection. During the ordinary course of business, this distribution of power generated a sense of nimble responsiveness to the immediate needs of individual communities. But in moments of crisis, this hyperlocalized control created pervasive inefficiencies in regional and state-wide coordination, as the act, which remained unaltered into the twenty-first century, left emergency-services coordination to the 566 individual municipalities across the state.[35] The act had profound implications in the organization of postdisaster relief and recovery in the aftermath of Sandy.[36]

As localism became further entrenched at the governmental level, new innovations in transportation were opening up the state to greater development and bringing more homeowners to the coast. In 1947, the State Highway Department began construction on the Route 4 Parkway. When funding for the project slowed three years later, the state legislature created the New Jersey Highway Authority, charged with creating and managing a high-speed toll road to run along the coast, opening access to the Jersey shore and contributing to economic, residential, and commercial development across the state. In 1956, the Garden State Parkway opened, extending 164 miles south to north, from Cape May at mile zero to Pascack Valley, near the New York border.[37] As the Parkway developed along the coastline, Governor Alfred Driscoll pushed through legislation for the creation of the New Jersey Turnpike, a high-speed artery running through the center of the state. The project, which was completed in a blistering twenty-three months, was funded on bond and repaid with revenue from tolls. By January 1952, the 118-mile road stretched from Bordentown in the south to Newark in the north.[38] The creation of these two cross-state roadways opened up access to the coastal areas of New Jersey, driving people to the region. The marshy shoreline and barrier islands, which once served as a natural buffer between the ocean and the built environment, became densely populated multiuse communities by the latter half of the twentieth century, exposed to assaulting storms.

When Hurricane Donna passed by Keansburg in 1960, it devastated the boardwalk community. Donna, which brought wind gusts as high as one hundred miles per hour and more than nine inches of rain to parts of New Jersey, destroyed beachfronts from Cape May, at the southern tip of New Jersey's coastline, up through Monmouth County and the Bayshore.[39] Bob Pulsch, who lived his whole life on the same property in Port Monmouth, was at a grocery store in East Keansburg when Donna hit. He had stopped in to pick up hamburger meat, and when he walked out, he said, the scene was out of a movie. Timbers were floating across the road. Waves ripped the tires right off the rims of his neighbor's truck. Cars ended up in the creek.[40]

Not long after Donna, a large section of the neighborhood was cleared in an urban renewal initiative, bifurcating the region along class lines. In 1969, Keansburg Township allocated $7.9 million to the Bayshore Hurricane Protection Plan.[41] Developed by the Army Corps of Engineers and the New Jersey Bureau of Navigation, the project expanded the width of Keansburg's beaches and added impressive—and unsightly—hurricane dikes along the waterfront. The plan served to create mechanisms for protection against coastal storms, but it had the unintended effect of blocking beachfront views for visitors and lifeguards alike, heightening the risk of accidents and creating a two-mile eyesore of a boardwalk.[42] Tourism continued to decline. Just a few years later, William Gelhaus sold the amusement park.

By the turn of the twenty-first century, New Jersey was the most densely populated state in the country, with 1,138 people per square mile.[43] Real estate and business growth transformed the coast into a densely populated tourist area, among the most developed shorelines in the world. During the months between Memorial Day and Labor Day, when seasonal residents and short-term

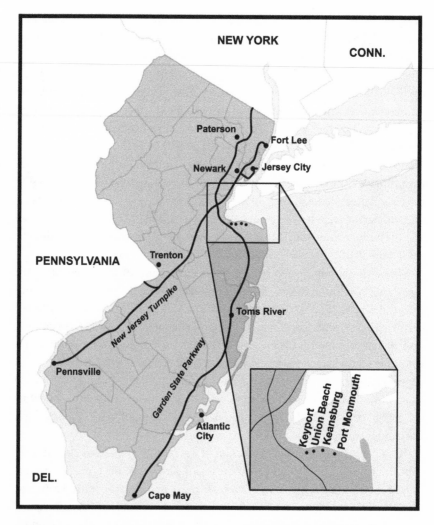

**FIGURE 1.1**   Map of New Jersey with inset of Bayshore. By Mark Lattanzi.

vacationers arrived, the Jersey shore became an epicenter of activity. In 2012, the year that Sandy hit, the tourism industry brought $40 billion to New Jersey, 7 percent of the state's total economy, with more than 50 percent of that coming from the four counties along the coast.[44]

But that investment was uneven. Though Monmouth County ranked among the highest-income counties in the United States, the towns along the Bayshore experienced marked economic decline.[45] In part, the area suffered because of its relative isolation from the rest of the county. "The Bayshore region draws much of its tourism from the local area," noted the Monmouth County Planning Board in 2005, "but many Monmouth County residents do not have easy access to the region and instead travel to the beaches along the Atlantic Coast. While Route 36 sees thousands of tourists every summer weekend on their way to the Gateway National Recreation Area on Sandy Hook and other shore points, few of them venture further west into the Bayshore communities."[46] This was, in no small part, because of the fractured beaches, where access was limited and often broken up by industrial areas, wetlands, and creeks and tributaries running into the bay.

In 2005, when the Monmouth County Planning Board developed its strategic plan for the redevelopment of the Bayshore, it highlighted the restoration of the waterfront as a critical piece of the region's strategic vision. Along the bay, there were more than one thousand acres of Critical Environmental Sites, the report read, so designated for their inherent sensitivity to environmental change. These wetland areas—which included 282 acres in the Bayshore Waterfront Park adjacent to Port Monmouth, 80 acres in Union Beach, and the entire 22-acre Keansburg waterfront—were particularly susceptible to the ongoing development of the shoreline and the reduction of open space in the region. "Beach erosion is an urgent problem that threatens the beaches and waterfront users," the report noted. "Flooding from coastal storms," the committee wrote, "is [also] of concern."[47]

That 2005 warning proved prophetic. Six years later, Hurricane Irene made landfall at the end of the tourist season. The Category 1 storm resulted in eleven deaths, two million power outages, and upward of $1 billion in damages across the state. Three days before Irene hit, on August 25, 2011, officials launched carefully coordinated emergency-management protocols. Governor Chris Christie declared a state of emergency. The same day, on the southern end of the coast, Cape May County's emergency management director, Frank McCall, issued a mandatory evacuation of the barrier islands. Similar orders came in Ocean County and Atlantic County on the twenty-sixth. Two days later, Christie announced the closure of the Atlantic City casinos and the Garden State Parkway. "Get the hell off the beach," he famously told residents and visitors in Asbury Park, on the Atlantic coast. In what *Washington Post* columnist Jennifer Rubin later called Christie's "Giuliani Moment," referencing the famed New York City mayor's defining presence after the September 11, 2001 attacks, the New Jersey governor implored beachgoers to "get out."[48]

In the weeks after Irene hit, these coordinated efforts across South Jersey, pulling together several counties and dozens of municipalities, were largely heralded. Across emergency-management systems, Irene was celebrated as a model of disaster preparedness. The National Weather Service proclaimed its forecasting and tracking an overwhelming success:

> Hurricane Irene tested the technical, human, and psychological resilience of citizens, emergency response organizations, decision makers, and the hydrometeorological capabilities of the National Oceanic and Atmospheric Administration's (NOAA) National Weather Service (NWS) personnel. The National Hurricane Center forecasted the track, landfall, and progress of Irene accurately and worked successfully with federal, state, and local emergency management (EM) partners to warn and protect those in the storm's path. NWS staff, in its coastal offices along Irene's track, worked in close partnership with emergency agencies to deliver accurate, clear, and compelling forecasts, watches, and warnings.[49]

And when NOAA identified areas of deficiency—technological gaps and risk of substantial service lapses, the need for enhanced social media reach and better collaboration with broadcasters, stronger partnerships with non-NOAA groups, and demands for access to mapping platforms—state and federal agencies worked to resolve these issues and strengthen infrastructure and capacity for the next storm.[50]

Though Irene caused substantial destruction on the Atlantic coast and along several of the interior rivers and creeks, on the Bayshore the storm was a bust. A few miles to the east of the Gelhauses' Keansburg Amusement Park, Port Monmouth's Adam Bixby and his family lost power for a week, but the water never got past the front lawn.[51] The same distance to the west, Union Beachers Millie Gonzalez (no relation to Linda) and her mother left their house to stay further inland at a friend's house in Cranford, and when they returned to the Bayshore, they were relieved to find their home untouched. They had no water damage and experienced minimal effects from the sustained winds. "There was more damage, technically, in Cranford," Gonzalez remembered, "with downed trees and water surrounding the area."[52] Union Beach was quiet.

Many of those living along the Bayshore were frustrated and felt like the government had cried wolf, creating unnecessary frenzy and causing needless stress. A year later, when forecasters started predicting another storm, some residents were reluctant to listen. As meteorologist Adam Sobel wrote of how New Yorkers prepared for Sandy, for those living on the Bayshore, Irene "cast a long shadow over government warnings."[53] Collette Kennedy's new neighbors in Keyport told her she was crazy for taking down her Halloween decorations in the days before Sandy made landfall. "They threaten us all the time about hurricanes," they said. "You'll learn once you live here never to get ready for any of them. They don't really come."[54] "I figured it would just be another storm," remembered fireman Glenn Perroth of Port Monmouth.[55] In Union Beach, Anthony Cavallo was similarly unconcerned. "My grandfather built this house in 1960. We never had a drop of water in our house, so I wasn't overly concerned with the storm even when I heard it was coming and it was going to be big."[56] Cavallo, like so many on the Bayshore, had grown accustom to the threat of storms. The region enjoyed a long tradition of waiting out the weather with the confidence of mid-Atlantic East Coasters, respectful of the power of the seas but generally sheltered from the worst of what that power could wield. "There was a certain complacency up in the northeast here, that this kind of stuff couldn't happen to us," Sister Sharon Kelly, program director of Keansburg's Bayshore Community Center, said.[57] The dissonance between governmental warnings and Irene's unrealized power had only amplified that sense of security and had made residents leery of giving too much credence to the prestorm panic.

Gary Szatkowski of the NWS said of the preparations for Hurricane Sandy, Irene "set us up for failure. I didn't want Hurricane Irene on the brain. I wanted people thinking 'worst coastal flood on record.' . . . It takes a lot to get people out of here."[58] This time is different, echoed CNN meteorologist Rob Marciano. "When you have trees with leaves still on them, this kind of wind and rain on top of that, you're talking about trees that are going to come down, power lines are going to be out and the coastal flooding situation is going to be huge." In short, he implied, Sandy would bring chaos in whatever form the storm took.[59]

On Friday morning, three days before Sandy made landfall, Szatkowski issued another briefing. "Confidence has increased," he wrote, "that the storm will have major impacts on our region."[60] Three hours later, Gerald Thornton, Freeholder Director of Cape May County at the southern tip of the coast, issued the first evacuation warnings in the state. Effective immediately, said Thornton, there would be a voluntary evacuation of all of New Jersey's southern barrier islands, those areas most susceptible to the predicted path of Sandy. Starting Sunday morning, he continued, the evacuation order would become mandatory. From there, the warnings escalated quickly. Just after 2:00 p.m., Governor Christie issued his own call for mandatory evacuations of the islands and other communities projected to take a direct hit from the storm. He told those municipal governments that they had free rein to do whatever they needed to prepare. "It's easier to ask forgiveness than ask permission," he went on. "Get done what you need to get done."[61]

On Saturday, two days before landfall, Christie crisscrossed the state to warn New Jerseyans of the ferocity of the oncoming storm. His day began at the Regional Operations Intelligence Office outside of Trenton, the state capitol.

From there, the governor traveled 60 miles north to East Keansburg for a news conference, and then came the mad 120-mile dash to the southern shore town of North Wildwood for a briefing at the Anglesea Fire Company. Taking the stage nearly an hour behind schedule and wearing the navy-blue fleece that would soon come to characterize his post-Sandy uniform, Christie told reporters that they were facing a potentially devastating scenario, with conditions far worse than anyone in the state had experienced the previous August during Hurricane Irene. It was time for decisive action. There would be a mandatory evacuation of all barrier islands from Sandy Hook on the northern end of the Atlantic coast to Cape May, beginning at 4:00 p.m. on Sunday. Toll plazas would be opened for free access to the Garden State Parkway and the Atlantic City Expressway so that residents could travel unimpeded. The Atlantic City casinos would shut their doors. There would be shelter beds for twelve thousand people in eighteen counties across the state. There was a plan in place to mobilize space for five thousand additional people, if needed. The entirety of New Jersey was under a state of emergency.[62]

Christie, often celebrated by his supporters for his take-no-shit attitude and criticized by his detractors for his bullish bravado, urged residents to take heed. This isn't the time to question the forecasters, he told them. It's not the time to focus on past storms. "How about we go by this rule?" he said to the room of reporters in East Keansburg. "Anything that looks stupid is stupid. If you think you're being overly clever but you know it's really stupid, don't do it."[63] Christie's emphatic warnings prompted residents to take notice. Up and down the shore, people in the evacuation zones began to make plans to leave their homes and head inland.

And then, just after 6:00 p.m. that evening, New York City mayor Michael Bloomberg took the podium at the city's Office of Emergency Management. "This is a dangerous storm," Bloomberg told the packed room. "And I think we're going to be okay. If things are the way it's planned and if everybody does what they're supposed to do, we will get through this very nicely." All city workers are expected to come to work on Monday morning as scheduled, he said. Commuters might encounter delays on the Staten Island Ferry. But, he predicted, Hurricane Sandy should be less damaging than Irene.[64]

Back at the Mount Holly National Weather Service office, Gary Szatkowski wasn't sure he had heard the New York City mayor correctly. *Get through it very nicely? With only ferry delays to contend with? Not as damaging as Irene?* His phone started ringing unabated. No one knew what to do with this new information. Journalists and newscasters couldn't make sense of these conflicting reports. In the wake of Bloomberg's disastrous press conference, the NWS forecaster felt he had no choice. It was time for a dramatic play. It was time to make it clear, once and for all, what the region was dealing with. He needed to be direct. This wasn't the time for prudence. He needed people to move.[65]

Szatkowski didn't sleep that night. How could he get residents to understand the dire potential of the oncoming storm when public officials were downplaying it? How could he convince people to listen to the evacuation warnings when most didn't and couldn't really understand what it would be like to look into the eye of the storm? In 2011, the NOAA meteorologists Chris Landsea and Eric Blake estimated that nearly 90 percent of people on the East Coast had never experienced a hurricane. That percentage was only increasing, with Americans converging on the coasts at a rapid pace. Until Sandy, the region had experienced only two mandatory evacuations in the previous forty years. "That's infrequent enough," said Szatkowski, "that people should have known we were serious. Still, I got that people weren't getting it. They were hearing conflicting reports, and the raging subtext of that conflict was 'Don't go anywhere.'"[66] He opened his computer and did, according to Miles, "what no meteorologist had ever done in the forty-two-year history of the National Weather Service: he wrote a personal plea and published it along with his noon advisory."[67] The typically measured Szatkowski urged listeners to take heed. "Sandy is an extremely dangerous storm," he implored. "If you think the storm is over-hyped and exaggerated, please err on the side of caution. . . . You can call me up [if it's a bust] . . . and yell at me if you want." He included his contact information at the end of the briefing for good measure.[68]

At 6:10 a.m. Monday morning, the day Sandy made landfall, the eye of the storm was 220 miles southeast of Atlantic City. Ninety-two minutes later, the area saw its first high tide of the day, and the battering surge spilled over the beaches.[69] Eighty feet of the city's boardwalk ripped from its moorings. Just up the coast, Tuckerton Beach, sitting on a pinprick of a peninsula on the southern end of the Barnegat Bay in Ocean County, experienced eighty-mile-per-hour winds. The entire town of Ocean City was submerged.[70]

One hundred miles north, the waters of the Bayshore were calm. Still, Angelita Liaguno-Dorr was worried. Known around town as Gigi, Dorr was a fixture in Union Beach. In 1999, she had opened the doors of Jakeabob's Bay. Named for the two Dorr boys—Jake and Bobby—the restaurant offered cold beer, hot steamers, and live music at the tiki bar overlooking the Manhattan skyline.[71] When Dorr initially heard about Sandy, she figured that at worst, the restaurant would have to shut down for another five months, recalling the 2010 nor'easter that had lifted the floors of the waterfront hotspot and blown out the back wall. "At first," she recalled, "I dismissed it . . . I said, 'it's fine, we're fine.' We called it 'spaghetti strings' because they kept [predicting] different paths. But then as the week kept going, it kept getting closer."[72] In the days before the storm, staff cleared the first floor of the restaurant, stacking things on the bar or balancing them on milk crates, making sure that everything was at least four feet off the ground.

And then they waited. To see how much rain would pour down, how much wind would blow through. To decide whether they should leave. By midday Monday, said Dorr, "the water was ugly. It was angry." At 3:00 p.m., they resolved it was time to go. "We could see the water. It just kept coming in and coming in."[73] They made a plan. They would drive inland to wait out the brunt of the storm. Then, once the high tide began to recede, they would come home and assess the damage. Dorr and her family packed up and made their way away from the beach, bracing for what they might find when they returned.

At 5:00 p.m., CNN news anchor Wolf Blitzer went live in anticipation of a scheduled 5:30 p.m. news conference from Christie. "The worst is yet to come from Hurricane Sandy," warned Blitzer. "Here's what we know at the moment. The center of this monstrous storm, which has brutally pounded much of the eastern seaboard of the United States, could come ashore this hour. New Jersey is bearing the brunt of the attack right now. . . . The powerful winds, the torrential rain, the storm surges, they are wreaking havoc from North Carolina all the way to Maine. The area of tropical storm–force winds extends almost—get this—a thousand miles." More than 765,000 people in seven states were already without power, Blitzer continued. Blackouts lasting for days could affect tens of millions more.[74]

When Christie began his press conference at 5:38 p.m., he announced the closures of sections of the Garden State Parkway and the New Jersey Turnpike, the two main arteries bisecting the state, along with forty-two state roads across thirteen counties. "For those of you on the barrier islands who decided it was a better idea to wait this out than to evacuate," he warned, "for those elected officials"—referring to Atlantic City mayor Lorenze Langford, who had told residents to find shelter on the islands, rather than evacuate—"who decided to ignore my admonition, this is now your responsibility. If you're still able to hear me, we need you to hunker down and get to the highest point in the dwelling that you are in. We will not be able to come help you until daylight tomorrow. Please try to hunker down and stay safe until then."[75] In short, he implied, residents were stuck until the storm was over.

As the governor issued his warnings, Michael Melfi was in his Port Monmouth yard, barbecuing sausages. His wife, Joann, had spent the day cleaning—more a product of her nervous energy than of any real need—and Michael had taken their daughters to the beach to see the waves. They were receiving regular messages from friends, calling on them to leave, but after unnecessarily evacuating during Irene, they saw no reason to go this time. At 6:30 p.m., a neighbor called with a more urgent warning. "By the time I left the backyard and got to the front door," said Michael, "I could see water coming around the street." At that point, he told Joann and the girls to go. He would stay home and take care of the house.[76]

Just before 7:00 p.m., the National Hurricane Center downgraded Sandy to tropical storm status. "We are now calling it Superstorm Sandy," a representative for the Weather Channel tweeted.[77] "But the lowering in status [is] no reflection of the power the storm still [packs]," noted Christina Ng for ABC News.[78] An hour later, after a week of anticipation, the storm finally made landfall just south of Atlantic City. At the time, maximum sustained winds were measured at eighty miles per hour. "Sandy's furious winds have already toppled scores of trees and electrical lines," the *Star Ledger* reported that night, "knocking out power for more than 1 million homes and businesses throughout the Garden State."[79] The storm was ambling north/northwest at twenty-three miles per hour.

Michael Melfi looked out the window, watching the water rise. It hit the first step. Then the second. *Maybe I'll be okay,* he thought. The water started seeping through the crawlspace underneath the house. That crawlspace was his insurance policy. It created an extra gap between the ground and the first floor. It should hold the water off, he hoped. Then the water started spreading across the floor. He thought about calling Joann. Instead, he rushed to bail out the boiler room. But it was useless. He sat down in a chair and started to cry. He knew high tide was at 8:30 p.m. All he could do until then was watch the water rise.[80]

# "PLEASE, SANDY, NO MORE"

Mary Jane and Roger Michalak thought they were prepared. They had stocked up on candles and bottled water. Roger had an ax and a hammer on hand, just in case they had to break through to the roof, the highest place available to them. A former beautician and a retired Dupont company man, the couple had purchased their Union Beach home from Roger's brother forty-seven years earlier, shortly after they married. The house was slab, with a carport elevated inches off the ground, then three steps up to the dining room and kitchen, and nine more steps to the upstairs bedroom and bathroom. In the almost fifty years that they had lived there, they had experienced their share of storms; they thought that they had seen the worst of what might come.[1]

The night that Sandy passed over, they sat together, listening to the gathering winds. As Mary Jane got up to use the restroom, she walked past the laundry room and noticed water leaking in. "Rog," she called, "there's water coming through the door." Roger told her to leave the door closed. And then he looked down and noticed that the rug below his feet was changing color. *Holy shit,* he thought. *It's coming.*[2]

Mary Jane hurried back in and looked around. Earlier in the month, she had gone shopping for an upcoming Christmas party and splurged on a new pair of dynamite stilettos. The box was getting soaked on the floor next to the television. "My shoes!" she cried. "My shoes, my shoes, they're ruined!" She rushed over and picked up the bag, hurling it onto the dining room table, where she thought the shoes would be safe. Roger couldn't help but laugh. *The couch is floating across the room and she's worried about her stilettos,* he mused. But soon, the dining room table was covered in water, too. Then the hutch.

"Roger, I think we'd better get upstairs," Mary Jane said. "We'll drown if we stay any longer."

Then the water reached their landing.

"We'll have to go and get up on the roof," she urged.

Roger picked up his ax and hammer and then paused. "Mary Jane, I'll never fit through the hole in the attic," he said.

She paused. "I guess we'll drown together."

The couple sat down on the bed, waiting for the water to wash over them. They had lived at the edge of the bay.

And then, just before the water reached the bedroom, it began to recede. They both let out a breath they hadn't realized they were holding.[3]

When Sandy made landfall in Atlantic City, the storm's winds swept up the coast and into the triangle of the Raritan and Sandy Hook Bays, shored by Staten Island to the north and the Bayshore to the south and pushing west into New York Harbor. This wedge, where the Michalaks found themselves, "compressed the incoming surge like a funnel, amplifying it until it reached the triangle's point," wrote Adam Sobel.[4] The Federal Emergency Management Agency (FEMA) estimated that more than ten thousand people were directly exposed to that surge.

The storm's timing intensified its destructive power. The full moon would have pulled tides 20 percent higher than normal on even the calmest of days, and Sandy crashed into the Bayshore right as that tide reached its peak. At its height, a wave topping out at more than thirty-two feet pulverized New York Harbor. In Manhattan's Battery Park, the surge reached nearly fourteen feet at 9:24 p.m., surpassing by more than three feet the old record, set during Hurricane Donna in 1960.[5] At the Gateway National Recreation Area at the eastern tip of the Bayshore, the storm surge was recorded at close to nine feet above normal tide levels before the station lost power. "Since the station failed and stopped reporting during the storm," the state Department of Environmental Protection noted in a 2015 assessment report, "it is likely that the actual storm surge was higher."[6] Between Battery Park and the Gateway National Recreation Area sat the towns of Keansburg, Port Monmouth, Union Beach, and Keyport, devastatingly exposed to the rising waters crashing along their shores. And the water had no place to go but inland.[7]

Just a mile away from the Michalaks, the water began rushing into Linda Gonzalez's home at 7:00 p.m. At 8:21 p.m., she and her family heard transformers

**FIGURE 2.1**  Woman fishing off the pier at Bayshore Waterfront Park in Port Monmouth, with New York skyline in the distance. Photo by Sharon Karr/FEMA. March 1, 2013.

popping all over the neighborhood. Then the power went out. Her grandchildren had gone to bed earlier, with glow-in-the-dark stars affixed to their ceilings and battery-powered tap-lights on their walls, token gestures designed to make them as comfortable as they could be with the violent winds outside. Her children finally drifted off to sleep once the worst of the storm had subsided—after her son-in-law had waded through four feet of water to put out the fire in his wife's car, and after they had watched the mattresses, boats, and rooftops floating down their street.[8]

Gonzalez couldn't bring herself to close her eyes. She knew she would need her strength to get through the next day, the next week, the next month. But there were police lights flashing down her street, neighbors walking around, and people yelling. Someone was trapped in a house down the block, she heard. More sirens. An ambulance. So much noise punctuating the postsurge eerie quiet. No, sleep wasn't an option.[9]

And so, by candlelight, she started to write. In verse, she chronicled the day of the storm: the darkening skies and the winds kicking up, her fear rising with the waves. In one stanza, she captured the anxieties of the entire Bayshore:

> Holding our breath that the water won't come in
> Wondering if the surge of water will end

Eight inches to go before it comes to the door
We all just kept saying, "Please, Sandy, no more."[10]

When she finished, she put down the paper, blew out her candle, and lay back down, thinking about the rooftops floating in the street, the father who walked down the sidewalk with his children on his shoulders because their house had been ripped away, the flash of transformers blowing, all cloaked in darkness, covered by the night. She replayed the scenes on continuous loop until morning, the storm raging in her mind even after the winds and surges had subsided.[11]

Eight miles to the east in Atlantic Highlands, Andrea Bulvid had decided to spend the weekend with her parents, just to be safe. The twenty-seven-year-old real estate paralegal lived in the same town, with her husband, Brian, and their ten-year-old daughter. When Hurricane Irene hit in 2011, the water had risen to ten inches below the first floor of their house. "We got through [it] by the skin of our teeth," she remembered. They considered staying in their home for Sandy as well, but then town officials came down her street with a bullhorn. "Get out," they called. "You have until 8 o'clock. Be out." They decided to take heed. On Saturday evening, the family walked down the street to her parents' house, just 120 feet away but raised higher off the ground. They thought they would be safe there.[12]

On Sunday morning, as Andrea and her parents readied the house, Brian, a contractor, made the trip to Long Island to pick up a generator—a favor from the supply house where he had a corporate account. He filled up his gas tank on the way back to the house and left his pickup in a nearby park, just in case they needed it. By the next evening, that park—and his truck—would be fully submerged in water.[13]

They lost power in the early afternoon hours on Monday, and then as the tide receded, the water levels began to drop. They took a breath, bracing for what was to come. "The water [went down]," said Bulvid, "but not completely. That let us know how bad it was going to be." The storm was sitting offshore, fighting back against the outgoing tides, pushing the water inland. Her father grabbed a measuring stick from the basement and carefully marked up the wall, ticking off each foot. When he got to the top of the stick—five feet from the floor—he wrote, "Oh, shit." That became their "oh shit" stick. They understood that if the water went above the "Oh shit" mark, they would be in real trouble.[14]

They stacked boxes, moved valuables to higher elevation, and placed the generator on the coffee table, hoping it would stay dry. Then they put the gasoline canisters in the bathtub. When they had prepared as much as they could, they sat down in the kitchen and waited. For a while, there was just wind. But as the tides rose again, the water returned. At first, they couldn't tell how high it was. Then they started hearing noises; the belongings they had so carefully stacked in the basement were floating to the ceiling and bumping against the rafters beneath their feet.[15] Then the water came through the floorboards, soaking the carpeting on the first floor. They decided it was time to move upstairs.

Earlier, they had stationed an inflatable kayak by the window, filled with life vests for all seven people in the house. They wanted to be near the boat, just in case. Andrea took her daughter and their dog to the second floor. Her mother and sister followed, toting a guinea pig and the family bird. At first, they sat in silence, listening to Brian and her father setting up the generator, checking on the gasoline, splashing around on the first floor. They started to sing, "to drown out the noise of the wind and the water, to take that edge off."[16] Andrea posted a photo of the upstairs group on Facebook, tagging her mother and sister. They wanted everyone to know where they were, just in case something happened.[17] Like the Michalaks, they braced themselves for the worst. Twenty minutes later, as suddenly as the water had surged through the floor, it began to recede. They took a deep breath and posted one more photo to Facebook.[18]

Back in Keyport, Collette Kennedy was sitting in her car, parked inside the attached garage of her one-story home. She had spent the early part of the evening collecting the debris that was falling down all around her property, worried

**FIGURE 2.2**  Photo from Andrea Bulvid's Facebook feed, used with permission from Bulvid. Her post reads, "We made it! Water on its way down. It came up about 6 inches into the first floor after it crested. Tomorrow will be a busy day." October 29, 2012.

that the loose refuse would crash through the front window of her house. In the middle of her living room, a pile was developing. A stop sign. A piece of her neighbor's chimney. The final time she went out, she could barely get back to her front door. Twenty minutes later, she heard the loudest sound she'd ever heard in her life. "I thought the air conditioning unit on the high rise building across the street from me blew off, but it was really a wall." The looming apartment complex included two eleven-story towers conjoined by a ground-level entranceway. The narrow open-air corridor between the two faced the bay, and the gusts sweeping off the water rushed through it with such force that they ripped eight stories of the brick façade from the face of the building, crushing the corridor. [19]

That's when Kennedy went out to the garage. She thought about going into the basement, but she had read on Facebook that houses were collapsing all over her neighborhood, and she knew that if that happened to her, she would be crushed. "It was the first time that I realized that I was completely alone and brand new to town, so if there were rescues at that point, would anyone know to come?" For the next six and a half hours, she sat inside her car, Facebook her only companion, assessing and reassessing her odds of surviving. *If a tree falls in the yard*, she thought, *it will probably hit the attic first. Then the garage. Then it has to get through my car to get to me.*[20]

As she waited, she watched her entire street transform into a countywide rescue operation. When the façade of the apartment complex had ripped off, the building lost power, cutting off the critical electrical supply for all of the residents, including those living in the senior center that occupied part of the space. "They had every responding town that they could get there, trying to get those 458 seniors out of the building . . . they had to carry them all down the steps."[21]

In Port Monmouth, Michael Melfi finally decided he needed help. He called Joann, who was staying at their friends' house nearby, and explained the situation to her. The house was filling with water. He had no way out. Their friends knew a local detective in Middletown, just a few miles away. "We're going to call Paul Shanley," Joann told Michael. "Just relax. We're going to call."[22]

But Shanley had bad news; Middletown had put a ban on rescues in the area. "Tell him to sit tight," the detective said. "I'll see what I can do." High tide came and went. The water inched up past Michael's chest. Finally, he heard trucks driving down his street. The detective had worked his magic, and the National Guard was coming for him. The soldiers dropped Michael off to a waiting Shanley, sitting in his car at a gas station on Wilson Avenue. From there, the two drove to the house where Michael's family was staying. Exhausted, Michael changed into dry clothes and went to bed. They thought the worst was over. It was the last full night of sleep Joann would get for several months.[23]

Five miles west, Cheryl Mara heard someone screaming outside her Union Beach home. She and her daughter were sitting in the living room, playing dice to pass the time after the storm took the power out early in the evening. Her two-year-old granddaughter slept in her crib nearby. When Mara heard the scream, she went to the front door. What she saw stunned her: a woman flailing at the end of her block, chest-high in water. Somehow, there was still no water in front of Mara's own house. "I'm yelling to her to come up but she can't hear me, or she's not responding. So, I turned around from that door, came back [to the living room] to grab my cell phone, which was on the couch." By the time Mara got back to the door to check on the woman, water had begun to rise over her front steps. Mara remembered the sudden shift: "It came in with a fury."[24] She woke the baby and ran to the attic, seeking higher ground as she knew to do in the floods of a storm. Her daughter corralled the dogs, and the cats followed them up the stairs. As the family took refuge in the attic, Mara realized that they were stuck. "We were trapped up there. If the water came in and stayed and came up, we were trapped." Not knowing how much water was covering the floor below, Mara called the police for help.[25]

Authorities were sending boats through the streets of her neighborhood, but their priority was to attend to the people stranded along the bay, those sitting on their roofs in danger of being thrown into the water. By the time they arrived at the Mara residence, it was after 11:00 p.m., and the water had begun to recede. At that point, recalled Mara sheepishly, "I was feeling foolish that I had called for help. But you know, I had my granddaughter up there, and my daughter.... I wanted them out, and my daughter wouldn't go without me." Even though the surge was abating and the moment of urgency seemed to have passed, when the rescue boats came they had no choice but to leave. They secured the pets in the attic, shut the door, and sailed down the street to the town hall.[26]

As the Maras made their way to safety, Gigi Dorr and her family were trying to get back to Jakeabob's, right on Front Street in Union Beach, at the water's edge. But they kept running into obstacles, downed trees and sparking power lines cutting off their route at every turn. Dorr tried to call in favors from friends on the police force, but everyone told her to turn back. The water was too high, they warned, the conditions too dangerous. Finally, the Dorrs relented and turned back toward Borough Hall. As they navigated the wreckage in the streets, they watched blown transformers light the night sky green.[27]

"We sat at borough headquarters from 11:30 p.m. to 2:30 in the morning," said Dorr. They were just waiting until they could return to the waterfront. "I asked twice if the building was still there, and they kept saying, 'We don't know.'" Finally, someone came in and announced that they would be able to access the beach-front following the storm's worst onslaught. Not knowing whether her bar was still standing was too agonizing to bear; Dorr had to see it herself. "They took us down," she recalled, "[and] we were driving over couches, toilets, dressers, trees, hot water heaters. . . . It was just a mess. It was like, there was cinder blocks, there was parts of buildings, there was doors. . . . It looked like the town blew up."[28]

She followed the officers onto Front Street around 3:00 a.m. and watched as they flashed their headlights on the restaurant. At first, Dorr was relieved to see Jakeabob's prominent teal roof still attached. But then she noticed that the building next door was completely gone. "There were no walls. There was no roof. There was nothing." It was a shocking sight. And then she heard a sharp hiss. She looked over and saw a utility worker frantically trying to repair a gas line. The chaos of the storm's destruction continued to grow even as the winds and waters receded. But there was nothing she could do. Dorr and the officers turned around and went home, waiting for the sun to rise and illuminate the full extent of the damage.[29]

When residents steeled themselves to leave their homes on Tuesday morning, they found themselves ill prepared for what they encountered when they opened their front doors. The devastation was enormous in Union Beach, Keansburg, Keyport, and Port Monmouth, the cities of the Bayshore wedge that had taken the brunt of the storm's force. Houses had collapsed in on themselves. Roofs were washed out to sea. Boats had piled high on top of each other, wherever the waves and the surge decided to drop them. Mary Jane and Roger Michalak found fish lying limp on their front lawn, nearly a mile away from the waterfront.[30] A six-foot wall of water had pummeled the Keansburg Amusement Park, sweeping rides across the neighborhood, the funhouse attractions standing out in stark contrast to the destruction all around. Three feet of sand filled the carousel. The Wildcat, the park's most famous roller coaster, lay in pieces.[31] Millie Gonzalez saw arcade machines floating down her sister's street, half a mile away.[32] Olde Heidelberg, the park's iconic hot dog stand, was destroyed beyond repair. Only the original tables—dark wood with marble tops, dating back to 1934, when the restaurant opened—were salvageable.[33]

Millie, sitting in the upstairs bedroom at her sister's Keansburg home, heard laughter.

"Someone is singing 'O Solo Mio' outside the window," her sister called from the first floor, "and I'm trying to figure out who it is."

"Okay," said Gonzalez.

"It's our father. He's in a rowboat."[34]

Their dad, who lived fifteen miles down the coast in Perth Amboy, had not been able to get in touch with them. He drove as close as he could and then

**FIGURE 2.3**    Damaged rides at the Keansburg Amusement Park. Photo by Liz Roll/FEMA. November 30, 2012.

unloaded the boat from the back of his truck and paddled over to make sure they were okay.[35]

Linda Gonzalez and her family decided to go outside in shifts; they couldn't let the grandkids see the devastation. When it was Gonzalez's turn to go, she headed straight for the waterfront. She walked slowly, crying. The smell—a mix of mud and seawater and crabs—turned her stomach. There were people everywhere, taking stock of the destruction. "What am I going to do?" she heard them wail. "I've lost everything." She shook her head. "There was just nothing left," she said. "You couldn't walk in the street without walking in a foot of mud and sand and debris and people's pictures and clothes and mattresses and sinks and refrigerators. . . . [The storm] took a house and blew it up [all along] the beachfront."[36] There was cracked pavement, signs bent in half by the pressure of the surge, a statue hit with such force that it split in two. "The surge of water that had to hit a small condensed concrete statue, I can't even imagine the force of the water coming in," Gonzalez later recalled. "It's supposed to be so solid. A house, okay, it's big and it's going to fall apart, but—that blew my mind. . . . It gives a whole new perspective of the force of the water and the forces of nature."[37] And then she got to Union Avenue. There on the water, just beyond the seawall, was half a house. The hundred-year-old structure, originally owned by a sea captain, had been sheared in half.

Gonzalez's Union Beach neighbors included James Butler's parents. The day after the storm, Butler made the four-mile trip from his own house in Matawan to his childhood home. The drive, usually only fifteen minutes, took three times that long. Officials hadn't set up roadblocks yet, so he was able to travel freely—if carefully—all the way down Brook Avenue, where his parents lived. Except the house was gone.[38]

"Right next to them, in the middle of the street, was a house that I didn't even recognize. I wasn't sure which house it was." The house had been lifted from its foundation, four lots away, and had swept down the street with such force that it knocked down everything in its path. "Like a battering ram," said Butler.[39] His parents' house had gotten in the way, and now there was nothing left. No walls, no sinks, no furniture. They found the attic halfway down the street. Everything else, they suspected, had been washed away in the early surge.

"My first thought . . . was [that] somebody had to have died." There's no way—no way—that people survived this. . . . People had to be dead, because their houses were just washed into houses." He became frantic, trying to get in touch with everyone he knew. He began hearing stories of people who swam out of second-floor windows, out of attics. But somehow, everyone was still alive. "I don't know how we got that lucky."[40]

Butler walked down the familiar streets, trying to make sense of what he saw. "The worst-hit area was my old paper route," he recalled. "I know those houses. I know the families that were in them." He had traveled to New Orleans after Katrina, had seen the devastation that such a storm could bring. He thought he knew what to expect. But this was different. For Butler, this one was personal.[41]

# "EVERYTHING IS GONE"

Anthony Cavallo and his family spent the night at the highest point in Union Beach: their church, Faith Chapel, with pastors Fred and Ruth Allen. There had been wind, some rain. The power went out. "We'd figured we'd just gotten a hurricane," he said. "We've had hurricanes before." They awoke Tuesday morning and began to organize themselves for breakfast. *Like a normal day*, Cavallo thought. But he knew it wasn't a normal day. By 7:00 a.m., he was restless. He and Fred walked outside to check on the neighborhood. "We're going scouting," they told their families.[1]

They drove down Union Avenue, taking in the scene. In the distance, he saw a small structure in the road. "I think somebody's shed blew into the street," he remarked.[2] As they got closer, he realized it was the second story of a house. They parked the car near Brooke Avenue and set off on foot. There, they encountered a man, standing in the road, crying.

"Have you seen it?" he asked them.

"Have we seen what?" Cavallo responded.

"The whole street's gone."

Cavallo and Allen turned the corner. "There was debris everywhere. Houses were just gone. We heard gas coming up from the houses." They decided to turn around. It was too dangerous. "One spark," he said, "and this whole thing's going to blow up."[3]

He wasn't concerned about his property at that point. Their house, his grandfather's "American dream," was three blocks off the water, after all. Instead, he focused on the obstacle course of debris that lay in front of him. "I hope I don't get a flat," he said.[4] They made their way slowly. He wanted to check on his place before they went back to the church. He assumed it would be a quick stop. Then they hit a checkpoint.

"Where are you going?" asked the officer on duty.

"To my house on Dock Street," he told her, "just to check everything out."

"Good luck," she responded.

"Good luck? For what?" he asked. "We don't get any water."

She let them through.

Cavallo and Allen turned onto his street, and then he saw it. "Everything in the house was turned over. . . . It was gone."[5]

His first thought was *I'm the one who has to break the news to my family.*

They made their way back to the church. Ninety minutes had passed by that point, and breakfast was almost ready. He walked inside and sat down. His wife, Jeanne, handed him a plate of scrambled eggs.

"It's gone," he said.

Gone? They didn't understand.

The house, he explained. "Everything is gone."[6]

Ninety percent of Union Beach flooded when Hurricane Sandy made landfall. Nearly every home—more than 2,000 of the 2,336 properties in the borough—incurred damaged.[7] As Molly Hennessy-Fiske of the *Los Angeles Times* reported, houses there were "beat[en] to a nearly unrecognizable pulp."[8] When the water abated, residents didn't know where to begin. Who do you call first? How can you initiate a claim when you don't have cell service? Should you carry debris out to the street? Should you take pictures? If you move anything, the insurance company won't know what you lost—but you can't live like this, while you wait for the assessors to come. "It seemed like you could sell information during that time," recalled Millie Gonzalez, "because people just didn't know what to do."[9]

For Andrea Bulvid, the woman who had waited out the storm on the second floor of her parents' house with an inflatable raft, just in case her family needed to paddle to safety, it was paralyzing. "I just stood there staring at my house," the twenty-seven-year-old recalled.[10] They got four feet of water. In their one-floor ranch house, everything at ground level was destroyed. Quickly, her extended family stepped in. Her husband's cousin brought the entire Monmouth University lacrosse team. "They gave me direction," Bulvid said. They began by packing up everything that hadn't sustained damage. Then they hung their waterlogged clothes on the fence to dry. At night, her mother-in-law scouted open laundromats to get everything washed. The system worked. They were able to salvage quite a bit that way. It was a start. Then she turned to the phone. "Who do you

**FIGURE 3.1** In Union Beach, this house was washed off its foundation, leaving only the roof in its place. The couple living there swam to safety. November 4, 2012. Photo by Liz Roll/FEMA.

look to for support?" she recalled. "Your power company? Insurance? FEMA?" There was no playbook for this one.[11]

At the Cavallo house, Anthony wandered from room to room, in a daze. He thought, *How do I do this? My grandfather built this house fifty years ago. There are too many memories, too many keepsakes. How do I sort through it?* "When you're throwing your life's treasures away, you have to stop and . . . look at every piece." There was a knock at the door. He walked downstairs to find Mennonite volunteers standing on his front step. "We will clean out your house," they told him. "We'll gut the floors, gut the walls, take everything out for you." Their generosity allowed him to find a path forward. "It was a godsend," said Cavallo. He invited them in, and they talked through what needed to be done. When they passed by his office, he closed the door. He wasn't ready to deal with that yet.[12]

With the help of the visitors, the family set to work. Those early days were long, exhausting. "You need to clean your house before the mold comes," Cavallo said. You need to try to salvage anything you can." There was no time to think or process or reflect. "You just go." Without power, they had no hot water for showers. At night, as the temperatures dropped into the forties, they crawled into bed, covered in the mounting layers of grime and sweat, and they shivered.

On Sunday, five days after the storm, Anthony hugged Jeanne. "I don't like being dirty," he told her.[13]

For the Cavallos and their Bayshore neighbors, suddenly the triviality of daily life came under scrutiny. What will I eat for dinner, when everything in my fridge is rotten? How can I open this tin of tuna, if my electric can opener doesn't work? Linda Gonzalez got creative, grilling up two pizza pies on their backyard barbecue.[14] It was a modest meal for the eleven people in her house, but it tasted good. Home cooking was a delicacy in those early days after Sandy.

Sometimes, said Iris Miranda of Port Monmouth, there wasn't time to think about food. The Mirandas had found shelter during the storm at a hotel ten miles inland in Edison. When they returned two days later, their property was almost unrecognizable. The walls were bubbling below the water line; the flooring was buckling and cracked. Outside, their six-foot fence was under water. There was a tree in their pool. The days that followed were long. There were times when she stopped to catch her breath and realized, "Oh my god, I have to feed my kids!" It made her angry, watching CJ, her ten-year-old, moving boxes or cleaning up trash—not able to be a kid. "Oh, did I want to scream. Oh, did I want to curse everybody out. I was so upset," she recalled.[15]

In Keansburg, seventy-one-year-old Henrietta Williams's biggest priority was finding a refrigerator. Williams had waited out the storm at home, frustrating her family members who were urging her to leave. Her whole block sheltered in place, ready to help each other when it passed. During the night, Sandy sucked her attic fan straight through her roof and tore up the wall that had separated her house from her neighbor. She had been on the same street—in the same house—since 1977. She lived with her dog and spent her days teaching art at the Bayshore Community Center or taking water aerobics classes at her gym in Middletown. She was independent, for the most part, and she liked it that way. But Sandy was different from anything she had experienced before.[16]

Williams would eventually have to attend to the damage, but first she needed to deal with her health. A diabetic, she knew that her life depended on finding a place to store her medication. She started by calling her friends to see if they had room in their refrigerators. No one had power. As she stood outside her home, feeling helpless, wondering what to do, a nun from a local parish came onto the block and asked if there was anything she could do. With the sister's help, Williams was able to get in touch with her nephew, who was powering his own refrigerator with a generator.[17] The small act preserved thousands of dollars' worth of medicine.

Across the Bayshore, gas shortages limited travel, and curfews meant residents had to be in their homes by early evening.[18] Bulvid said, "The National Guard was checking IDs. . . . My mother-in-law tried to bring food down for us and she got stopped at the firehouse and I had to pick her up and take her in."[19] At night, recalled Cavallo, local officers, sheriffs, and National Guard members patrolled his Union Beach neighborhood, safeguarding against potential looters. They were under lockdown. The police presence made them feel safe, Cavallo said. Not secure, but safe.[20]

In those first hours and days after the storm, Bayshore residents felt lost. There were so many decisions to make. No one could find their footing. Everything was out of their control. "I think everybody was waiting for somebody to roll in and just kind of take charge," said James Butler. "And that person, I guess, doesn't exist."[21] The person with all the answers may not have existed. But in that moment, New Jersey seemed to have a close substitute in Chris Christie. For the nation, Christie came off as a no-nonsense leader who wasn't afraid to raise his voice or cross partisan aisles to make things happen. Sandy turned Christie into America's governor, and for a time, the shining light of the Republican Party, a presidential hopeful for 2016. For many Bayshore residents, even those who hadn't supported the governor in his bid for office, he offered a glimmer of hope. Months later, Christie would face harsh criticism for what his detractors perceived as his focus on the tourism infrastructure along the Atlantic coastline over the hard-hit year-round residential communities. But in those early days and weeks following the storm, he made those communities feel heard.

Long seen as a red stronghold in a blue state, Monmouth County has voted majority Republican in all but four presidential elections since 1900.[22] More than 62 percent of voters punched the ticket for Christie as a first-term governor in 2009, a 31-point margin over the Democrat John Corzine, compared to the governor's 3.57-point margin statewide. So, it was no surprise that residents heralded the governor's leadership in the wake of the storm. It was his presence, said Adam Bixby, a long-term Christie supporter. "This is about being from New Jersey and taking care of your town." Christie did that.[23] "Christie has the right perspective," reflected Bulvid. "He's down the middle of the road. . . . We need somebody to get us back on track that's going to be realistic."[24] That was Christie. "He went out like a bull in a china shop," said Bob Pulsch.[25] That was just what New Jersey needed.

For those who could access it, Christie had a near-constant presence over the airwaves. "There are no words to describe what so many New Jerseyans experienced over the last twenty-four hours," the governor said in his first press conference, the morning after the storm. "I'll first say to all of you, especially those out there who are facing loss, devastation, and the heartbreaking reality that your home may be gone: we are with you."[26] And New Jersey residents believed him. The governor toured the state, talking with victims. He pressured federal lawmakers to pass swift relief through Congress. The morning of October 31, he issued a declaration postponing Halloween, a relief to Linda Gonzalez: "Who wants their kid walking around seeing all this devastation?"[27] On November 2, he announced plans to ration gasoline, trying to create order out of chaos. New York City mayor Michael Bloomberg followed suit six days later. When residents didn't know where to start, they looked to Christie for answers. "Don't wait for your insurance people to tear down your walls, because they won't," Bixby heard the governor say over the hand-crank radio he had purchased in his pre-Sandy preparations. He took the warning to heart and ripped everything out before the mold could settle.[28]

Even Christie's detractors gave the governor high marks for his presence and voice in the immediate aftermath of the storm. "There's a lot of things about Christie that I don't like," said Maureen Piasecki, "but I do think he did go above and beyond, and he did the best he could in the situation at hand."

"I think he's doing a great job," her husband, John, followed up, "and I'm a Democrat. . . . I might even vote for Christie, I like him so much."

"Oh, stop!" Maureen laughed.[29]

"I think the storm did change my opinion of Christie a little bit," reflected Sister Kathleen O'Halleran, who served at Project PAUL, a nonprofit social services agency that opened in Keansburg in 1980. "I think he shoots his mouth off too much, but I have to give him credit for that. . . . I may disagree with a lot of his policies that he thinks are good for the people, but in these instances, yes, I think he did show that he was here for the people of New Jersey."[30]

These sentiments of those along the Bayshore fell in line with perceptions of the governor across the state. Christie's approval ratings shot up in the wake of Sandy. A two-part Farleigh Dickinson University poll reported a 21 percent jump, from 56 percent before the storm to 77 percent in the weeks that followed.[31] Many New Jersey residents were particularly struck by the governor's willingness to put partisan politics aside during the recovery. A steadfast and loud supporter of the Republican nominee, Mitt Romney, Christie made it clear after the winds slowed and the surge abated that his role in the upcoming presidential election would be taking a backseat to Sandy recovery. "This administration, at the moment, could give a damn less about Election Day. If you hear the things that I just talked about and the devastation that's been visited upon this state, I am sure that while the national election is obviously very important, the people of New Jersey at this moment would be really unhappy with me if they thought for a second I would occupy my time thinking about how I was going to get people to vote a week from today. . . . So, I don't give a damn about Election Day. It doesn't matter a lick to me."[32]

On October 31, the governor greeted President Barack Obama on a runway in Atlantic City and escorted him on a tour of some of the hardest-hit areas around

**FIGURE 3.2**    President Barack Obama and Governor Chris Christie tour storm damage. October 31, 2012. Photo from the Barack Obama Presidential Library.

the state. Conservative media outlets around the country condemned Christie for his apparent love fest with the Democratic president.

But for New Jersey residents, the leaders' ability to put politics aside was laudable.[33] "It was a wonderful model," said Sister Kelly. "I think to some extent, maybe some people saw him as an effective leader, where maybe they hadn't before."[34] James Butler agreed. "I was actually very impressed with seeing . . . two very different sides in politics at least agreeing," said Butler. "A lot of people took reassurance in the fact that these two seemed concerned and listened to the people, because . . . that's what people want all along. Stop talking about the houses and showing us the images, and just get down and talk to the people. They'll tell you exactly what's going on and where they are. Enough with the rubble, and more about the family of four."[35]

That bipartisan tour of the state's beach towns foreshadowed the harsh criticism the governor would later face. At the time, though, much of the critique was directed at Obama, condemning him for his decision to visit with residents of Belmar and Brigantine while Union Beachers stood idly by. "He could have stayed the hell out of here," said Cheryl Mara bitterly. "Just to show up here, make it look good, that doesn't impress me. Get your hands out there and figure out what's going on. . . . Obama didn't know Union Beach existed. Christie did."[36]

"He didn't come to my town," echoed Glen Perroth, an elevator operator from Port Monmouth, of President Obama. "I didn't see him. The governor came to our town, though."[37] Linda Gonzalez of Union Beach felt similarly. "I know he went in by helicopter, and I know he can't be in a million places . . . but it's not the same as getting down on the ground. If Bon Jovi can do it, the president should be able to do it, and Bon Jovi did it."[38]

On November 3, Christie's helicopter touched down at Bayview Elementary School in Port Monmouth. From there, he climbed into an SUV and traveled to Port Monmouth Fire Company No. 1. The governor spoke with volunteers and residents, listening to their stories, bearing witness to the suffering they had endured over the previous five days.

Of course, unless they were there at Fire House No. 1 that day, few Bayshore residents ever heard the governor's remarks. With widespread power outages persisting, residents had no access to television, and even if they did, most were too busy to watch. "If there wasn't someone knocking," remembered Cheryl Mara, "you didn't hear about it."[39] Michael Melfi had the same experience. "There was little contact with anybody," he said. It was nearly a week before he could reach his employer to let the company know why he wasn't at work. Without access to local or national news coverage of the storm and its aftermath, "we just lived it as it happened in our community"[40]

"We didn't get to see the coverage [of the storm]," said Bulvid. News outlets came and went even before her power was restored. "The storm came. They warned you about the storm. Then the storm left. They covered the devastation, and then they were on their way. . . . It's old news."[41] There were helicopters flying overhead, said Linda Gonzalez, but residents on the ground "couldn't see what was going on." It was frustrating. "[And then], when we finally got TV and saw all the devastation, that was like going through it all over again."[42]

Social media became a critical resource. Though cell service was spotty, within a few days of the storm, those with smartphones were able to reconnect with the world. It became a way to get news, to share information, to direct resources, and to find community in a time of destabilization and chaos. Before Sandy, Cheryl Mara hated her cell phone. But without home internet, without power, without cable and phone service and television, she embraced it. "That's all I have now," she said, "my iPhone."[43] For many, iPhones became a vital link to the outside world. Sal Cortale, executive director at Project PAUL, had long ago gotten rid of his home landline. His cell phone was all he had. Before the storm, he bought a power adapter and kept it in his car. In his preparations, he downloaded the Facebook app and followed New Jersey State Information, Holmdel Patch, and the state emergency groups.[44] It was how he stayed connected to the Keansburg community he served and how he found the services his organization now desperately needed to rebuild.

The cellular network wasn't perfect. Cavallo saw wide gaps in coverage. "You would get a blip on your phone," he said, "and the internet was working for ten minutes. You can get a message out . . . then the Internet was going. Then eight hours later, the Internet came back on."[45] Joann Melfi experienced the same. "We were able to get a text," she remembered, "but sometimes we weren't getting a reply until a day or two later, because that person's provider was down, and they weren't receiving what we were sending out."[46] Still, the ability to log in to Facebook kept neighbors connected, even when they were forced to leave their homes and their communities for extended periods of time. Millie Gonzalez, who lived with spina bifida and was generally confined to a wheelchair, wasn't able to return to her Union Beach home for three days after the storm. When she did, she found it completely devastated. Her hospital bed, her shower chair, and her manual wheelchair were ruined, corroded by the saltwater that poured into her home. She lost a month's worth of medical supplies. It took over a year for her and her mother to rebuild.

Social media became her lifeline and Facebook her eyes and ears in the community. People reached out from around the country. Within twenty-four hours, friends in the disability community started a virtual crowdfunding campaign to raise money for her. Portlight Inclusive Disaster Strategies, an organization that works specifically to provide disaster relief to people with disabilities, connected with her on Facebook. "I didn't know who they were. I don't know how they knew who I was."[47] But they found her, and they offered her a grant to get through those first few weeks after the storm.

In those early months, being online kept her connected. Friends from Union Beach posted regularly with updates on the cleanup and the resources that were becoming available. Friends around the country saw Union Beach on TV and reached out through private messaging. "Until Superstorm Sandy happened," Gonzalez reflected, "Union Beach was barely on the map. . . . But then all of a sudden, people started to recognize it as one of the places that was affected by the storm."[48] This national spotlight on Union Beach brought together a virtual community that helped temper the physical isolation Gonzalez experienced after the storm.

To be sure, the attention on the town wasn't always welcome. The Princess Cottage, one of the most iconic images of Sandy's destruction, was located in Union Beach. Prior to the storm, the 150-year-old house, just off the bay, had never flooded. When the current owner, Jon Zois, decided to evacuate, he was confident that he would have a home to return to when the winds calmed. He and his girlfriend came back the next day to discover that their house, the same one Linda Gonzalez had seen when she walked outside the morning after the storm, had been shorn in two.[49]

**FIGURE 3.3**   Union Beach's Princess Cottage. Photo by Liz Roll/FEMA. November 12, 2012.

Before long, footage of the property was showing up on TV. Reporters camped outside. Images went viral. Then came the gawkers, outsiders who would drive by and take photos of the destruction. This disaster tourism infuriated Andrea Bulvid. "These cars that were coming down the street . . . you couldn't even get one car through—the road was so narrow because the piles of garbage were just insane." *Get out of your car and help us*, she wanted to tell them. *Don't sit and stare.*[50]

But the self-serving voyeurism may have been worth it for the movement of voluntarism, galvanized by the national media attention, that brought much-needed energy and resources into the devastated community. Strangers got in their cars and drove to New Jersey to help. Churches held clothing drives and fundraisers. Money poured in from around the country, thousands of small donations that funded food pantries and baby supplies and small emergency kits. Gonzalez recalled the text she had sent to donate ten dollars to the post-Katrina relief efforts nearly a decade earlier. "That just [got] sent to my bill, and my bill's ridiculous anyway." It felt insignificant, she said. "But somebody in New Orleans got a box that said Emergency Kit that my ten dollars probably helped to pay for."[51]

Those donations did more than fill in the financial gaps for Union Beach. Residents there felt seen and supported, said James Butler. "[The town] was very lucky. . . . In some ways, it almost pitted town versus town." "Oh, Union Beach; they talk about the half house and they've got all this help," someone would say. "But what about Keansburg?" "There wasn't a unifying New Jersey effort to get word out."[52] Some felt that disparity acutely. Port Monmouth's Iris Miranda remembered turning to her husband after a long day of hauling furniture and flooring out to the curb. She had heard about the influx of support coming into Union Beach. It had to make its way down the Bayshore to them, right? "Eddie, I know this help is coming," she told him. "They're going to come help us. I know it's coming." It never came. "We didn't have the orange sticker on our door," she said, referencing the labeling system first responders used to mark homes as unsafe for occupancy. *They must be okay*, she imagined volunteers saying. "Bull crap, we're okay."[53]

Those feelings of invisibility were magnified on December 12, 2012, when performers came together for a benefit concert at Madison Square Garden in New York City. Headliners included Alicia Keys, Billy Joel, the Rolling Stones, Roger Waters, Kanye West, and Jersey's own Bon Jovi and Bruce Springsteen. The event raised more than $30 million from ticket sales alone. Port Monmouth's Michael Melfi listened to the whole show. Brooklyn. Queens. Staten Island. He was keeping track of the towns that got airtime. "They got to Union Beach, and from that point on, they didn't mention any other town on the Bayshore. They went right to the Jersey shore." He turned to his wife. "Guess what, hon? We're forgotten already."[54] Maureen Piasecki agreed. Union Beach may have had more bayside bungalows, vulnerable to the storm's winds and surge. It may have taken the biggest hit. "[But] we all got devastation. . . . I think [media outlets] needed to focus a little bit more on the fact that everybody along the whole shoreline, from Sandy Hook to Keyport, took a beating."[55]

The impact of the media attention for Union Beach had a compounding effect. As the external aid served to galvanize the community, local residents took up the charge as well. Within a week of the storm, Beachers were using Facebook to create networks of relief within the town. Anthony Cavallo watched proudly as his daughter and her friends created an online clothing bank. "I have an extra pair of sneakers," one person posted. "I've got a pair of shorts you can have for gym," offered another. "It started happening with the kids," said Cavallo.[56] And then adults joined in as well. Rather than waiting for official relief to arrive, they were crowdsourcing much-needed material services. And just as important, they were claiming their own voice in the recovery—and rebuilding the psyche of the community as well. "Right around that time," Cavallo remembered, "was when some mysterious guy found a washed-up Christmas tree and set it up."[57]

# "YOU CAN'T WASH AWAY HOPE"

James Butler couldn't sleep. After a full day at work and a long shift, he should have fallen into bed that night. Instead, he felt wired. He turned on his computer, logged on to Facebook, and started to write: "What I learned in Union Beach (Quietly while everyone's sleeping)." He began just after midnight on November 9, 2012, eleven days after Sandy hit. In part, he wrote for his friends and family, those with whom he was connected on the social media platform. He wanted to give them a glimpse into the cleanup in his community.

He also wrote for himself, to try to make sense of what he encountered and experienced. Butler used social media as so many did in those weeks following the storm: to connect, to process, to help, and to grieve. What followed over the next two hours were nearly two dozen separate posts, a series of discrete observations and reflections from his night of helping families sift through their lives. They appeared in quick succession—a stream-of-consciousness recounting, something his network could take in as he had throughout the evening—and revealed his own thoughts and the responses his musings elicited in real time. By the time the night was over, a nugget of a plan to bring his community back together had begun to take shape.

"'Let's see if we can help this lady find some clothes her size,'" he wrote at 12:56 a.m., recounting a conversation from earlier in the evening. "'She's wearing a leopard print top, with orange leggings, and I think those are actually pink leg warmers. She must need a lot of clothes.'"[1]

"'Um, she's a volunteer who didn't lose anything in the storm,'" he continued, playing out the other side of the conversation. "'She always dresses like that.'"[2]

"There's an audible moment in some conversations now where the choice seems to become more tears or just a glassy eyed joke about how it could have been worse joke [sic]. 'I always hated that ceiling fan anyway.'"[3]

"When you open an upper cabinet and tide water still drips out a week after the storm you get an even clearer picture of just how much water was in this house," he noted at 1:31 a.m.[4]

The post with the most responses came at 1:45 a.m. "It's tough to get a Beacher to accept help they need. There's a lot of pride packed in a square mile." Eleven people reacted to that one.[5]

"I seem to have slept better cold and in the dark than I do now in comfort," he wrote at 2:03 a.m.[6]

And finally, at 2:05 a.m.: "Every time I pass that artificial Christmas tree in a bag on the side of that field I'm tempted to set it up." It was just a passing thought, like all the others. Five people liked it. The next morning, two people offered casual comments on the post.[7]

"Good idea, set up tree for donations for kids only, to make sure Santa arrives," one friend commented the next morning. "Maybe toys for tots can help."[8]

"James the Christmas tree idea is a great [sic]," wrote another. "Thanks for all you are doing."[9]

And that was all. Just a late-night Facebook binge when he was too tired to fall asleep.

For the next three days, Butler drove past the artificial tree, sitting inconspicuously in a trash bag at the appropriately named corner of Jersey Ave and Shore Road. On the fourth day, he stopped. He wrestled the tree from the bag and looked it over. There was no stand, so he drove the four miles home and cobbled one together. He thought that eight screws would be enough to stabilize the tree. "It turns out," he posted two months later on Facebook, as he recounted the effort, "[that] a wet artificial tree is heavy and hard to set up while trying not to be seen in the dark."[10] When he got back to Union Beach with his makeshift stand, he noticed a woman walking away from the corner. In the dark night, he found a red string Christmas ball, damp and fraying, resting on a branch.[11]

He finagled the newly adorned tree into the stand. It tilted a bit, but it would have to do. He was almost done. His hands nearly numb, Butler pulled a piece of poster board from his car and started to write.[12]

> Dear Sandy,
>
> You can't wash away hope.
> You only watered it, so more
> hope grows.
>                 Signed,
>             "UNION" Beach

He wasn't satisfied. It had to be perfect, he thought. He stashed the first board in the trunk of his car and started again.[13] "I wanted to send a message to [Union Beach]," he reflected. "I had seen the weight of the destruction first-hand, and the reoccurring image throughout town was despair. I knew we needed hope, but I felt like we were still drowning in the storm water. I tried to word an inspirational message that reassured my town that Hope wasn't lost."[14]

Butler wasn't sure what to expect, but people in the neighborhood took notice. The next day, photos of his new project began to show up on his Facebook feed, friends wondering where it had come from and who was responsible for setting it up. One post revealed that tree had fallen down.[15] That evening, he returned to the corner of Jersey and Shore to secure the base. "It was still a bit wobbly, so I improvised and looked for something to use as support. It was all there around me—driftwood. Long pieces that had been washed up. Another sign from the storm I could use for a better purpose."[16] Butler arranged the waterlogged wood around the tree's base to weigh it down. This time, it held.

**FIGURE 4.1** The Union Beach Hope Tree. December 2012. Photo by James Butler.

The Union Beach Hope Tree became a symbol of the Sandy recovery.[17] Butler's efforts emerged as part of a coalescing network of individual homeowners, volunteer coordinators, and relief workers coming together to respond to the immediate needs of Bayshore residents. Neighborhood pride, the impulse to keep busy, and the slow pace of bureaucracy pulled the community together, sharing in grief and rallying to rebuild. In those early days and weeks, neighbors worked alongside out-of-state volunteers, who flocked to New Jersey from across the country. Filling the gaps in the official recovery efforts, this informal infrastructure mitigated the effects of the storm for the most vulnerable and formed a critical support base at ground zero of Sandy's destructive path.

In the weeks that followed Butler's fly-by-night landscaping, Union Beach residents began talking about the tree. On November 17, Chuck Seelinger and his daughter added a gold ball to the branches and a yellow star on the top. On Facebook, Seelinger issued a challenge to his neighbors. "On the side of my house on Jersey Ave, someone has stood a Christmas tree that washed up in the storm. . . . Let's see how fast that tree fills up."[18] The original red string ball never came back—"Every time I visit the tree I look for that ornament, hoping for its return," lamented Butler—but others did.[19] In the weeks that followed, a local business donated waterproof signs to stand next to the tree. Beacher Cindy Luminoso sewed the words "UB Strong" onto a skirt and draped it around the tree's base. Before long, Butler's original sign made its way to the front door of Gigi Dorr's Jakeabob's. Students from the Memorial Elementary School and the Daisies of Girl Scouts Troop 61041 offered handmade ornaments. A neighbor hung lights, and someone else ran an extension cord to plug them in. Most of the bulbs still worked.[20]

In November, Butler took to social media again with the intention of chronicling the life of the tree. He opened a new profile—username UB Hope—and from there, he created the UNION Beach HOPE Tree page. "Then I had people messaging me [about the new profile]. . . . *How did you hear about this? What's going on here?* Then people started friending the UB Hope [page]."[21] It had taken on a life of its own—and Butler rolled with it, eager to do whatever he could to foster community in his hometown.

Updating the new page became habitual. Sometimes he wrote three or four times a day, messages filled with hope and photos of the tree's branches, by then heavily adorned. Before long, despite his best efforts, he was known around town as Mr. Hope Tree.[22] And then came the gift cards, donations from far away, which Butler delivered in secret around the neighborhood. The first went out on December 1, little more than a month after Sandy hit:

> Hope sometimes comes in small, rounded packages.
> If you need it—use it!

If you know someone that needs it more—Pass it on!
Signed, UB Hope.[23]

He created a special photo album just to document the cards. "Be careful when you leave your driver's window open as you check out the UNION Beach HOPE Tree," he wrote that afternoon. "You never know what might float in." He wanted to inspire everyone—those who could help and those in need of help. It hadn't been his goal when he first erected the tree, but unexpectedly he was bringing the community together.[24]

The second gift card came a day later, fifty dollars to Target for "another Union Beach Supermom . . . displaced from her home while raising some amazing kids including a kid on both the autism and awesome spectrum," Butler posted. "Hope will sometimes find you in the strangest of places. "If you need it → use it! If you know someone that needs it more → Pass it on! 'When the world says, 'Give Up,' Hope whispers, 'Try it one more time.'"—Anonymous. Signed, UB Hope."[25]

"Gift card #3," Butler posted on December 4. "Hiding in the Union Beach Library. Wanna know where?" The card was tucked into Edith Hamilton's *Mythology*, at the story of Pandora. One resident responded to the post. "Wish they helped us like this, we have a family of six and lost everything, don't even know how we're going to have Christmas. We are in a hotel and have to be out on the 12th with nowhere to go. Everyone was helping in Keansburg the first two weeks then disappeared. It's unreal. Well, god bless you and keep up the good work." Butler—as the anonymous administrator of the page—responded quickly. "I may know someone that can help a little but it will cost you—one ornament for the tree. I don't care if it's a paper plate decorated by your kids. Let me know when you get to the tree." Butler got to work, and within hours, the person who responded to the *Mythology* photo found a gift card of his own, hidden in an elf hat on the back of the tree. "Utah Sends Hope," it read.[26]

Butler was having fun. The next week, he tucked a card into a copy of *Images of America: Union Beach* at the local Barnes and Noble. Then he stuck one into the arms of a snowman standing next to a Christmas tree in a neighbor's yard. One resident took note of Butler during his delivery. "Watched this tonight in disbelief," she wrote on Facebook. "Amazing what you do."[27]

"I was spotted?" Butler responded. "I thought I was slick and pulled it off unseen."

"I did point it out to my thirteen-year-old son and husband and we all watched for the miracle to happen, hoping the family who took it pays it forward when able."

"I'm going to start wearing disguises."[28]

Two hours later, the recipient posted as well. "I passed it forward to someone who needed to buy stuff for her kids for Christmas and it made her cry. Thank you for all you do."

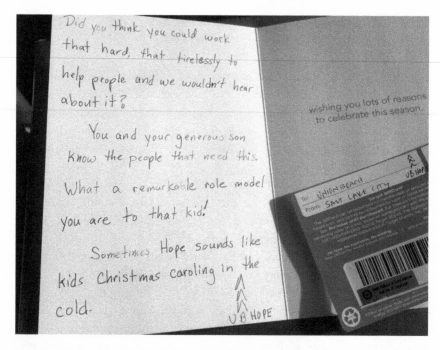

*Did you think you could work that hard, that tirelessly to help people and we wouldn't hear about it?*

*You and your generous son know the people that need this.*

*What a remarkable role model you are to that kid!*

*Sometimes Hope sounds like kids Christmas caroling in the cold.*

*UB HOPE*

*wishing you lots of reasons to celebrate this season.*

**FIGURE 4.2**   One of James Butler's anonymous deliveries. December 15, 2012. Photo by James Butler.

"Then the card found the right person," wrote Butler. "Thanks for being part of it.... There are so many stories like that out there that I would never be able to reach on my own. I'm so proud of this community that while dealing with their own cleanup are trying to help those that lost more. The gift cards won't fix their house or get them everything they need but it's a little help and a little hope that people need."[29]

He solicited the chief of police to deliver one of the cards; he asked a former mayor to hand off another.[30] One day, he slipped a note to the cashier at a local business, asking her to apply the card toward the next person in line. On Christmas Eve, he conspired with a clerk at the local Kohl's to get a card to its intended recipient. "I went to a funeral this year for a Union Beacher that passed away far too young," Butler reflected. "There's been a lot of that this year. I saw a sibling of theirs at Kohls. I was only in there to see if I could find a few ornaments. The gift card was donated anonymously at the library from a person that had lost a child earlier this year. It seemed like the perfect match."[31]

It became contagious. In February, he delivered a card to a family struggling to maintain the daily rigor of school and work with the pressures of rebuilding. "There may be days where you feel forgotten. That the rest of the world has just moved on. But there are so many people that think about you, and root for you, and hope for you. If you need it → use it! If you know someone that needs it more → Pass it on! Signed, UB Hope."[32] In March, Butler brought a donated twenty-five-dollar Walmart gift card to the Holmdel Barnes and Noble. Appropriately, he hid it inside a copy of Shel Silverstein's *The Giving Tree*—bottom shelf, fourth copy back. "Hope should sometimes take you by surprise," the card read. "How can I resist a book about a tree that gives much more than it receives? If you need it → use it! If you know someone that needs it more → please pass it on! Signed, UB Hope." The card was found, according to Butler, by a family mired in the bureaucratic red tape of storm recovery and working every day to get back home.[33]

Butler's hope tree emerged at a moment when many Bayshore residents found themselves flailing, frustrated by the slow pace of relief, angered by the bureaucracy of aid, confounded by the insurance adjusters, the jargon, and the piles of paperwork. These small acts of solidarity and kindness softened the devastation. In what seemed to so many like a profound vacuum of leadership, this collaborative spirit of voluntarism forged deep and lasting connections.[34]

Along the Bayshore, streets filled with debris, making it nearly impossible to navigate through neighborhoods. Power outages meant communication channels were inconsistent. Gas shortages created barriers to statewide travel. Temporary housing was nonexistent, forcing relief workers to set up residence an hour away in Pennsylvania, limiting their time on the ground as fall turned to winter and usable daylight became a precious commodity. Four months after the storm, only 4 percent of towns reported that they had received financial assistance from FEMA.[35] Donations from national nonprofit organizations like the American Red Cross accounted for just 2 percent of overall contributions in the aftermath of Sandy.[36]

As they waited for aid from official channels, communities came together to fill in the gaps. In Keyport, Collette Kennedy spent the days following the storm helping the 458 senior citizens who had been evacuated from the building across the street from her house to the local elementary school, Keyport Central School, which was being used as a makeshift shelter. She would travel to the closest operational grocery store and pick up staples for some of the residents staying there. She went to their apartments in search of medical equipment. She assumed that the Red Cross and federal assistance would step in, but she and her neighbors soon felt that they were on their own. The local first responders—the Keyport EMTs (emergency medical technicians) and Office of Emergency Management—became the heroes. The National Guard and the Salvation Army came relatively quickly; FEMA, a while later. But the local team couldn't wait, so they set up a shelter in town.[37]

Three days after the storm, Kennedy began taking the overnight shift at the ad hoc shelter. She worked from 7:00 p.m. to 7:00 a.m. for the following two weeks, as long as the site was open. Her aim was to help the volunteers with kids to try to reclaim a sense of normalcy. With Kennedy covering the nights, her colleagues could work during the day and then return home to their families.[38]

It was an intimate job, and she saw people at their most vulnerable. The school had been built prior to the enactment of the Americans with Disabilities Act building regulations, so there was limited accessibility. The bathroom stalls weren't wide enough for wheelchairs and walkers. The toilets were too low to the ground. People who had previously lived independently now needed support. Kennedy would help them get from the overcrowded sleeping spaces to the bathrooms in the middle of the night and then help them get changed. "There [was] a lot of trust that had to happen right from the get-go, for people to feel comfortable with some stranger helping them go to the bathroom." The shelter manager worked to foster that trust by prohibiting the use of cameras on the grounds. He didn't want residents to feel like someone was capitalizing on their suffering.[39]

Once the Keyport shelter closed, Kennedy found other ways to stay involved in the relief and recovery. In January 2013, she was nominated to the town's Environmental Commission. In that capacity, she pushed for new flood mapping and elevation plans and greater communication between the local, state, and national environmental preparedness programs. She attended FEMA meetings and reported back, becoming an advocate for those whose lives were too disrupted by the storm to participate in the planning process. "It was one less meeting they would have to sit through," she said.[40] She also joined James Butler's HOPE team, distributing donations to local residents in need of support.

Four miles east of Kennedy's Keyport shelter, Keansburg's Project PAUL had suffered substantial storm damage. Founded in 1980, the longstanding community organization operated a food pantry and a thrift store, with the mission of serving the poor, alienated, unemployed or lonely people of the Bayshore region. Executive director Sal Cortale explained, "We [provide] clothing, money to help people pay rent, food."[41] For thirty-two years, the organization on the front lines of need in Keansburg. And then came Sandy—and suddenly, Project PAUL needed help, too.

When Cortale woke up the morning after the storm, he tried to prepare himself for the damage he might find. He made his way carefully from his home in East Freehold to the operation's headquarters on Carr Street, traveling along sixteen miles of surface roads, dodging debris and refuse the whole way. When he arrived, he saw that the first floor of the thrift shop had filled with more than three feet of water. Everything—the three commercial refrigerators, the furniture, the air conditioning unit, the food—had been lifted off the ground and reposi-tioned when the water receded. The organization lost its entire inventory at the furniture and thrift stores. There were cars sitting perpendicular to the sidewalk, having floated along as the surge rushed through the streets. Arcade games from the Gelhaus's amusement park had washed up alongside the building. Cortale's truck driver was idling on the sidewalk, wary of the several inches of water still filling the road. *What do we do now?* he wondered. *Who's going to help us?*[42]

Though the organization's infrastructure was down, Project PAUL's key per-sonnel were ready to work. Sister Nancy Herron, one of only three paid staff members—all on "priestly salaries," said Cortale—lived in the convent at St. Anne's Parrish, a few blocks farther inland. The water hadn't reached the convent. Their driver, too, had been spared from the flooding.[43] The following day, Sister Kathleen O'Halleran, who had served the organization for twenty-four years, was able to make it over. When she had awoken at her Union Beach home the morn-ing after the storm, she thought she was on an island. "I couldn't get out of the house," she said. The water was still up to her waist. Twenty-four hours later, it had receded enough for her to get out into the neighborhood. "I waded my way down [to the convent], and then from there we started going over to the high school."[44] After that, she went to Project PAUL.

The skeleton crew put in twelve-hour days, six days each week. Because their usual volunteer corps was mired in their own cleanup, the responsibility fell largely on Cortale, Herron, and O'Halleran in the early period of the recov-ery. Over the next several weeks, more and more people showed up. Soon, there were more than fifty people on hand, working day and night to rebuild.[45] It was a Herculean undertaking.

Project PAUL's power was restored within the week, but when it came back on, it blew out a phone line, compromising service for several days. Though the insurance company resolved Cortale's claims quickly, finances were still tight.[46] The organization lost substantial revenue during the months that it was closed, money that staff relied on to operate and pay for insurance policies. Local and national media outlets followed the Project PAUL story closely. "We were the group that was always helping," said Cortale, "and now we were damaged, so we needed to get ourselves better so we could help others [again]."[47] It was a ready-made public-interest story, and the public responded, sending private donations to get the organization up and running again. By Thanksgiving, it was semi-operational, serving dinner to more than 100 families. At Christmas, it gave away 1,200 toys. Finally, in mid-February, Project PAUL reopened its doors to clients.[48]

Like Project PAUL, local religious communities partnered with faith-based organizations around the country to provide substantial support in the days and weeks following the storm. In Union Beach, the Gateway Church of Christ became a community hub, offering not only a spiritual foundation but a material one as well. Carl Williamson, Gateway's thirty-two-year-old pastor, had founded the church with his wife, Ashley, only a year earlier. They held services at the community space of the Holmdel Senior Center, just a few miles south of Union Beach. The day after the storm, one of the church leaders visited the Williamsons with a suggestion. "You know, we don't need these supplies," the man told Carl and Ashley. He suggested that they look to Union Beach instead.[49] The Williamsons got to work, calling on Ashley's mother, Dawn Adcock, in Nashville, Tennessee. Adcock reached out to the city's Churches of Christ Disaster Relief Effort, and within days, they had a truckload of supplies heading toward New Jersey.[50]

Meanwhile, Dorr was antsy. There was nothing she could do to save her beloved Jakeabob's, so she sat at Borough Hall in Union Beach with a deep need to be useful. "What do you want me to do?" she pressed Mike Harriott of the Office of Emergency Management (OEM). "What do you want me to do?" They were awaiting a clothing delivery, and Harriott suggested that she fold the clothes. "No, no, no, I'm not going to fold clothes," Dorr persisted. She wanted something bigger. She needed to make an impact. Harriott relented. "I'm going to go speak with the borough administrator." That afternoon, Dorr first learned the name Carl Williamson. "He's coming with a tractor-trailer full of supplies on

**FIGURE 4.3**   Volunteers from North Carolina Southern Baptist clean out apartments flooded during Sandy. This image is reflective of volunteer-based organizing across the state. November 30, 2012. Photo by Liz Roll/FEMA.

Friday," Harriott told her. "Okay," said Dorr. "So, I'll meet Carl." The OEM manager passed along Williamson's phone number. Dorr called him immediately.[51]

On Friday morning, less than seventy-two hours after Sandy struck the Bayshore, the truck from Nashville arrived. It was loaded with food, cleaning supplies,
blankets, and pillows—$90,000 in relief, the first to reach the area. Williamson
and Dorr got to work, setting up a donation center in the Holmdel Senior Center. By 5:00 p.m., every single thing had been claimed. Two days later, another
truck arrived. Before long, Dorr's Jakeabob's employees showed up to work the
center. They reached out to the local community, posting on Facebook, inviting
residents to come. "How they did it, I couldn't even tell you," recalled Dorr. "But
they did it."[52] It felt like a trial by fire. "Can we do this?" they asked. "Can we do
that?" Each question led to more questions, and rarely were there ready and reliable answers. "I was thinking to myself," Dorr said, "'Isn't there a handbook for
this stuff? Don't I drop it in a black box and it tells us what to do?'"[53]

Still, the facility became a fixture in the community, a hub for residents to
come together, to escape the frenzy of the recovery, to slow down and catch
their breath. "It was unbelievable," recalled Dorothy Gajewski, who had lived in
Union Beach with her husband Robert since 1988.[54] They had everything, echoed
Beacher Karen Kiely, a single parent who had finished renovating her home not
long before Sandy hit. "They had all kinds of cleaning supplies. They had bleach
and they had gloves and they had those white outfits to put on [Tyvek suits]. They
had sponges, and [mold remediation] supplies.... They had hot coffee and bagels
and donuts all the time. I would take my granddaughter almost every day and
we'd go over so I could get a hot cup of coffee and bring back a couple bagels for
the family."[55] Dorr and Williamson had created an anchor for a community that
had lost its footing. "That was the beginning," said Dorr. And Williamson, she
reflected, was her blessing. Soon, they were calling themselves the preacher and
the bar owner.[56] "A bar owner and a preacher wouldn't be the closest of friends,"
Anderson later recalled. "But now, we are family."[57]

Dorr applied that same community-minded commitment to her plans to breathe
new life into Jakeabob's. Knowing that it would take extraordinary effort—and
comparable funds—to reopen in their original location, she turned her attention
to finding a temporary home for the restaurant. She rented the old Seven Days
Bar and Grill on Union Avenue, half a mile inland and twenty feet above sea
level. Then she needed a name. She sat down one night with Jakeabob's former
manager, who, along with her daughter and parents, was living in Dorr's basement with her. At first, she wanted to incorporate her last name into the restaurant. But then she paused. We should collect doors, she decided. "What do you
mean, look at doors?" the manager replied. Union Beach residents were cleaning

up—hauling debris and remediating mold and sifting through waterlogged family relics. Dorr's idea was to ask homeowners for their soggy, rotting doors. They would restore them, refinish them, and then incorporate them into the aesthetic of the new restaurant.[58]

Before long, Dorr and the manager had collected dozens of them. They set up shop in the new space, cleaning, treating, and painting the doors, and then transformed them into tabletops and dividers, each displaying the address of its original home. "In the kitchen," said Dorr, "it's not table 1 through 20, it's 404 Shore or 910 Harris."[59] On the walls, they hung pictures of Union Beach before and after the storm. There was a spot for James Butler's original Union Beach Hope Tree sign, the one he had discarded because "it had to be perfect."[60] They found a home for the carved wooden signs that had been salvaged from the original restaurant after the storm. One, from the old tiki bar, was secured in a sand-filled flowerpot. "It weathered the storm," Dorr said. "It tells a story. What we've been through."[61] The new place, dubbed Jakeabob's Off the Bay, was an homage to the nostalgia of the small beach town and to the resilience of a community battered and beaten.

As word spread throughout the neighborhood of Jakeabob's resurgence, community members wanted to help. In February, Melissa and Mary Mancini organized Paper Doors for Gigi, a fundraiser to offset the costs of the renovations. Others donated decorations to adorn the walls of the new restaurant. Someone

**FIGURE 4.4**  Gigi Dorr shows the new doors displayed in Jakeabob's Off the Bay. March 26, 2013. Photo by Rosanna Arias/FEMA.

offered to make a new sign. Once again, Dorr's efforts were bringing people together, demonstrating the resilience of the Bayshore, creating something better than the sum of its individual parts. When Dorr opened Jakeabob's Off the Bay in April 2013, the Hope Tree Panini was one of the most popular items on the menu.[62]

This powerful coalition of de facto first responders embarked on a community-wide campaign to respond to the material and emotional needs of Sandy's victims. Working alongside official relief organizations, they were on the front lines of the recovery, triaging need, offering emotional support, staffing the third shift, and serving as the local institutional knowledge base in a time when much of the material and personnel support was coming from out of state. But the breadth and depth of need was overwhelming. And that broad-based response was short-lived. As the immediate disaster response gave way to a protracted and plodding recovery, market forces moved in, unmasking inequalities across the state and leaving Bayshore residents feeling impotent when confronted with the uneven pace of change and the shifting priorities of relief.

# A MODEL OF DISASTER PREPAREDNESS

When Adam Bixby and his family first bought their home in Port Monmouth, they looked through flood records on the property dating back to the 1970s. They wanted assurance that they would be safe in a storm, but more than that, they wanted to ensure that they would never have to deal with insurance adjusters, renovations, and rising premiums. "I don't mind paying a little bit of flood insurance," Bixby remembered thinking at the time, "but I don't want a history of flooding, because that's just a nightmare."[1] To their relief, there were no claims on the house for the period during which the township kept records. The family took out the requisite coverage when they applied for their mortgage—the federal government requires this for properties in designated hazard areas if there is a loan attached—but they figured it was purely for show. "We'll never get flooded," they thought.[2]

The Bixby house was one of the 365,000 primary residences in New Jersey that incurred damage during Sandy. For some, the destruction was too severe, the cost of rebuilding too high. More than 21,000 renters were forced to relocate.[3] The 1968 National Flood Insurance Program (NFIP) created a public-private partnership through which insurance companies offer flood insurance to property owners in vulnerable areas, but most homeowners only purchase a policy if their bank mandates coverage as a condition for borrowing against the house. In New Jersey, as of 2016 only 17,309 properties carried such coverage, out of roughly 350,000 exposed to potential hurricane storm-surge damage.[4] Many of those homeowners without NFIP policies simply could not afford to rebuild.

For those who stayed, the post-Sandy recovery became a rabbit hole of insurance wrangling, FEMA claims, and grant applications. The months and years after Sandy were occupied by a never-ending cycle of unanswered phone calls, piles of paperwork, and paralysis, as they navigated a system that seemed to them ill prepared to handle the severity of the storm and ill equipped to contend with the emotional and physical toll that the recovery had wrought.

The Bixbys were among the first to wade into the bureaucracy of aid. Unlike many who were affected by the storm, they had had the foresight and capacity to bring their insurance paperwork with them when they evacuated to Adam's brother's house. As soon as the water receded, Adam filed a claim. After that, he recalled, "It was just kind of a mad dash. I was getting inventory of everything. I immediately started taking pictures . . . because I knew the insurance company would want to see it as is." Their next step was to contact FEMA. "Within a day," said Bixby, "we already had a case." The agency deposited funds into their bank account for temporary housing and instructed the family to contact local hotels to see if they were taking in Sandy victims. Of course, everyone else was calling, too, and rooms were filling quickly. One receptionist told Bixby that they had a wait list a thousand families long. "That was one of the most anxiety-inducing feelings that I have ever had in my life."[5]

The Bixbys got lucky. Adam's brother knew the owner of the Blue Bay Inn, a twenty-seven-room boutique hotel in Atlantic Highlands. The Blue Bay's phone system was down after the storm, and calls weren't going through. Through the family connection, the Bixbys were able to secure a room. The family moved in that week, and they stayed for the next five months, joining the inn's other temporary residents displaced by the storm. Staff played with the kids. Management brought in presents at the holidays and arranged a special visit from Santa. They held a party.[6]

Once the Bixbys had secured temporary housing, they were able to turn their attention back to their own home. They got estimates from contractors for the renovations that would be required. They contacted home lifters for bids and awaited confirmation of how high they would have to raise the house. The insurance adjuster arrived four days after the storm and commended Adam for his thorough accounting. Six weeks later, the family got the numbers. The adjuster estimated that they had lost nearly 90 percent of the value of their house. The insurance company told them that it would match the contractor's estimates, covering the costs to rebuild, if not all of the contents inside the house.[7] In those early weeks, it seemed like everything was going smoothly.

There were so many claims to file and so many policies to keep track of. Of course, there was FEMA—everyone knew they should contact FEMA, Bixby thought. And insurance—they had to call insurance. But which one? There was the private homeowner's policy, and that broke down into structural claims and content claims—the appliances, the furniture, the clothing, the toiletries, the medicine, the food in the fridge. Then there were flood claims, all backed by the NFIP. Those got more complicated. Was the damage caused by rain? By wind? By surging waves? There were private adjusters, who worked for the insurance companies themselves, and public adjusters, who were lay people who had received ad hoc training in the wake of the disaster so that they could serve as intermediaries between individual clients and the companies that were charged to protect them. Those public adjusters, Gigi Dorr said, were crucial. "I would never, ever, ever, ever walk a step without one."[8]

Anthony Cavallo's flood insurance agent finally showed up on Thanksgiving, three weeks after Sandy hit. That visit marked the beginning of eight months of wrangling with his assigned private adjuster. Finally, in June, the company told Cavallo that the policy wouldn't cover the damage to his home. "The reason [the] house cracked in half is because of the water pressure that pushed the house," the insurance company told him. "But the front half sunk two inches and twisted. The engineer feels that that could be from the moistening and loosening of the soil underneath the foundation. In turn, [Cavallo's] adjuster said, 'That's called erosion, and we don't pay for erosion.'" They said he was stuck; there was nothing they could do.[9]

No one wanted to accept responsibility for the damage. Homeowners insurance adjusters blamed flooding for the damage, while property claims were refused because, agents said, the damage was caused by flooding. Allstate denied Dorothy and Robert Gajewski's initial homeowner's claim, directing them to go through their flood insurance policy. "No, we were here," Robert pleaded. "We rode out the storm. The shed, the screen room, all the fencing, all that came down before it even started raining." Allstate held firm. Flood insurance, they told him. What could the Gajewskis do? They made the call, and then waited five weeks for the new adjuster to arrive.[10]

They had adjusters and contractors out to the house. They brought in six engineers. Allstate's flood-claim office treated the project as a repair, telling them that the damage wasn't severe enough to warrant replacement. Others disagreed. "All the engineers. . . [said] that it was not safe to live there," said Dorothy.[11] Her nephew, a contractor, told them that if someone kicked the back door, the entire garage would fall down.

Still, they followed the adjuster's instructions and prepared the house for renovations. They spent $7,000 on cleanup, bringing in people to demold, pull out all the nails, and strip the studs. All the while, the couple, at sixty-six and sixty-nine years of age, lived nomadically. They spent twenty-four days at a Comfort

Inn on FEMA's tab, until the agency's paperwork requirements became too cumbersome. From there, they moved in with their daughter, eighty miles away. And then, on February 19, almost four months after the storm, they got a letter from Borough Hall, demanding the removal of the structure. "The township will not issue permits for any repairs to the standing structure," it said. Dorothy and Robert sent the notification to Allstate and FEMA. Nothing happened.[12]

The Gajewskis' experience was all too common. Extended delays, poor coordination, conflicting information, and miscommunication stymied their ability to move forward in the process of rebuilding. Disaster response in the aftermath of Sandy suffered from a federal emergency-management system that privileged homeland security over natural hazards. Those living along the Bayshore experienced the effects of those priorities firsthand.

Until the middle of the twentieth century, emergency management in the United States was coordinated on an ad hoc basis, with Congress allocating resources for discrete relief efforts. Disaster and emergency response fell on local municipalities and funds largely came from local coffers. It was not until 1950, against the backdrop of the burgeoning Cold War and global nuclear anxiety, that the legislature established the first comprehensive Disaster Relief Act, creating a permanent fund of federal resources to aid in disaster recovery. The law mandated that the federal government play an active role in disaster planning across the country. Still, for the next two decades, local authorities continued to bear the overwhelming cost burden and the responsibilities of implementation. As the journalists Christopher Cooper and Robert Block wrote, "In the early days, direct federal rebuilding money was used only to replace federal government buildings."[13]

In 1969, though, the immense destruction of Hurricane Camille prompted a reimagination of federal disaster relief, and for the first time Congress directed resources to individual homeowners and private businesses. The storm, which killed 143 people along the Gulf Coast and caused $950 million in damage in Mississippi alone, was one in a series of devastating hurricanes and earthquakes in the 1960s and 1970s. This string of natural hazards spurred renewed public interest in disaster assistance and prompted increased pressure on the federal government to respond.[14]

And respond it did. On March 31, 1979, President Jimmy Carter signed Executive Order 12127, officially creating the Federal Emergency Management Agency. FEMA, Carter pledged, would be "independent, apolitical, and adequately funded."[15] The new organization consolidated more than one hundred federal agencies, all loosely focused on disaster preparedness, and placed them under the directorship of John W. Macy, Jr. A career civil servant, Macy began his career in Washington in 1938 as an intern at the National Institute for Public

Affairs. He served as personnel director for the US Atomic Energy Commission from 1953 to 1969 (with a brief retreat from Washington from 1958 to 1961) and ultimately became the president of the Corporation for Public Broadcasting and the Council of Better Business Bureaus before being appointed to run FEMA. Though Macy had limited experience in disaster management, as a Washington man he was well-versed in organizational development. His integrated emergency management system—commonly referred to now as the "all-hazards approach"—was premised on holistic and far-reaching planning to develop tools that could be applied to any disaster situation, including natural hazards and civil-defense emergencies. The policy proved effective in responding to events such as the Three Mile Island nuclear accident in 1979 and, a year later, the eruption of Mount St. Helens and the Mariel boatlift, with its ensuing surge of Cuban refugees.[16]

Though Macy's approach drew praise from the communities affected by these early FEMA initiatives, the inaugural director was shown the door in 1981, following the election of Ronald Reagan. The Republican president prioritized nuclear preparedness over natural hazards, and his choice for FEMA director reflected those shifting administrative aims. With Louis O. Giuffrida at the helm, Cooper and Block wrote, the shrouded "black-budget" agency came to be characterized by "nuclear survivability programs" with "'crisis evacuation' plans to herd residents of some four hundred American cities into remote rural areas, where they would wait out a missile attack from Moscow."[17]

Giuffrida's time with FEMA was short-lived—the militaristic leader resigned in September 1985 amid growing scandal—but by the time of his departure, the resources allocated to nuclear scenarios outnumbered those allocated to natural hazards by twelve to one.[18] The nation would see the ill effects of such priorities in 1989, when Hurricane Hugo struck the South Carolina coast, and again in 1992, when Hurricane Andrew collided with South Florida. In both instances, FEMA's inability to respond in a timely and meaningful way proved disastrous for the local communities affected by the storms. In 1992, those effects were felt in Washington as well. The timing of Hurricane Andrew—just three months before the presidential election—laid bare the shortcomings of the agency under the George H. W. Bush administration. The president lost credibility with his once-reliable bloc of Dade County Republicans.[19] For the first time since 1976, the county swung left in the November election. Though Bush ultimately took the state—the first time Florida had supported a losing candidate since 1960—the unexpectedly tight race pushed Florida into the national spotlight as a critical swing state, which has remained into the twenty-first century.

FEMA was at a crossroads when President Bill Clinton stepped into the White House in January 1993. Disaster experts across the nation questioned whether the United States would be better off without the floundering agency, whose public reputation trailed only that of the Internal Revenue Service. Clinton sought to revitalize the organization. He put it in the hands of James Lee Witt, the former director of Arkansas's Office of Emergency Services, where he had served when Clinton was governor of the state. Witt's modest background in disaster management made him the first FEMA director with any disaster experience at all.[20]

Witt made it his mission to return the agency to its original all-hazards approach. First, he cut black-budget programs. Then, he worked with Senate leaders and the top managers in the agency to redirect budget dollars from nuclear preparedness to natural hazards. He began with disaster response but quickly rewrote the mission of the agency to focus on planning, prevention, and mitigation. FEMA's regional offices worked with local and state leaders to evaluate place-based realities and develop protocol accordingly. With each test, Witt proved himself a capable and competent leader, sending out rapid-response teams while mandating constant streams of communication from Washington to the local offices. By the mid-1990s, FEMA was garnering near-universal praise. Halfway through Clinton's first term, Kathy Kiely of the *Arkansas Democrat Gazette* called Witt "by far the biggest Arkansas success story in Washington."[21]

"I've never seen such a turnaround in an agency," said Patricia McGinnis, president of Washington's Council for Excellence in Government.[22] Lee Helms, director of the Alabama Emergency Management Agency, proclaimed, "I think there has been a total restoration of FEMA. Witt has cut out the red tape; there's much less bureaucratic nonsense and much more responsiveness to the state's needs. As we say in the South, he's got a head full of sense."[23]

But all that began to change when, just after 9:00 a.m. on April 19, 1995, Terry Nichols and Timothy McVeigh parked a Ryder rental truck filled with explosives in front of the Alfred P. Murrah Federal Building in Oklahoma City and blew it up. The attack killed 168 people, injured 680 more, and caused more than $650 million in property damage.[24] More significantly, it awakened the nation to the first major post–Cold War human threat: terrorism on US soil. President Clinton declared the event a federal emergency and Witt responded swiftly, activating eleven of FEMA's Urban Search and Rescue Task Forces and sending 665 first responders to assist in the search-and-rescue operations. Witt later called it his most difficult disaster experience. "The hardest thing was going in that building, meeting with search-and-rescue teams every day and seeing what they were going to, what was happening to those people," he reflected. "I was out there for thirteen days ... there's some tough memories there."[25]

This wasn't the first time the nation had experienced an act of terror on US soil—just two years earlier, members of the militant Sunni Muslim organization Al-Qaeda had detonated a truck bomb in the basement of the North Tower of the World Trade Center—but Oklahoma City marked a dramatic shift in the federal government's response to terrorism, globally and domestically. "In the past year, the country witnessed a re-emergence of spectacular terrorism with the Oklahoma City bombing," noted a 1995 Federal Bureau of Investigation report. "Large-scale attacks designed to inflict mass casualties appear to be a new terrorist method in the United States."[26] A year later, Congress passed the Defense against Weapons of Mass Destruction Act. Legislators urged Witt to fold antiterrorism into FEMA, but the director worried that such a shift would jeopardize his longstanding commitment to the all-hazards approach.[27]

After Sandy hit, Michael Melfi visited the FEMA office twenty times. At first, the agency offered temporary housing assistance, covering the Melfis' stay at a Holiday Inn. "But we would have to check in for four days, and then check out for three, and come back Monday." The Melfis knew that the situation was unsustainable. Eventually, they walked away. "When they tell me I can go somewhere for six months," Michael told Joann, "then I'll go. Otherwise, we're going to stay at my sister's."[28] He took a leave from work so that he could direct his energy toward rebuilding. "They wanted to fire me," he said, "because I took off more time than what I had. But what am I supposed to do? When the insurance company or the banks want paperwork, I have to get it. . . . If I waited until my one day a week to do all the paperwork, I'd still be doing it and I'd have no money to fix my house."[29] The bank released the money in January. It took another three months for contractors to come.

"I feel fortunate," he reflected, "because I had two insurance policies. But people here that lived the American dream, worked all their lives, bought their homes, paid it off, they don't need insurance, and now their homes were wiped out and nobody's helping them." It was September, eleven months after the storm, by the time the Melfis' house was completed.[30]

Like the Melfis, Iris Miranda and her family received an initial subsidy from FEMA. The agency deposited $3,200 right into her bank. These initial subsidies were a quick fix for families displaced by the storm, with the amount determined by the number of people living in the household. It was efficient, neat. It seemed too easy. The Mirandas realized quickly that it was. Without heat and hot water, they needed to move out of their home. Hotel rooms filled as soon as they opened, so FEMA officials gave them a list of apartments. Iris and her husband visited every one. "We don't take pets," one place told them. "We're not outfitted for kids," they heard from another.[31] Many property managers required them to sign a six-month lease. But they didn't want a six-month lease. They just needed a little bit of time, a temporary solution until the heat was working, until their water was turned back on.

So, they moved to Staten Island. Iris's cousin had just bought a house there, and he had a fully finished basement. But because they had no rent to pay, FEMA couldn't help them. There were no funds for gas, no funds for tolls. "It [would have been] a lot less than paying for an apartment," said Iris. Insurance was no better. "We had to get a public adjuster," she said, "because [they were] giving us so much work." Every day for six weeks, she drove her kids back to Port Monmouth, trying to maintain a sense of normalcy as best she could. "I sat in my car for six hours, waiting for them to get out of school," she said. The costs were mounting quickly. By the time the family's insurance check finally cleared, they had spent all of their funds. "We had no money left by the time insurance paid . . . and the insurance doesn't cover everything. Whoever tells you insurance covers everything, they're lying."[32]

Their flood insurance premiums skyrocketed, from $537 annually before the storm to $3,000, and then to $5,000. In the spring, the company told them that they would need to fill in their basement or risk even higher rates. "They considered it a living space," Iris said. What could they do? They filled in the basement. Their policy dropped below $3,000—"which I guess is better than $5,000," she mused.[33]

Meanwhile, Adam Bixby's luck had run out. By March, FEMA was telling the Bixbys that the agency wouldn't cover their room at the Blue Bay Inn any longer. "You have to find a rental place," FEMA officials said. But there were no short-term rentals, and the Bixbys didn't want to sign a yearlong lease. So FEMA cut them off, and after five months in a hotel, they moved back home. They settled into life on the second floor of their house, and they got creative. Without gas or heat, they had no stove or hot water. They ate shelf-stable meals, boiled water, and took sponge baths. "Like camping out in our own house," said Bixby.[34] That lasted for six weeks, until the contractor came to lift their property.

Their flood insurance provider told them they would need to go up five feet to meet the revised flood protection elevation guidelines. The aim of lifting a house is to protect the living space from all but the most severe flooding—as FEMA defines it, the sort of damage brought on by a five-hundred-year flood.[35] The Bixbys decided to go up seven feet, raising their home sixteen feet off the ground. They did so in part to safeguard against another Sandy—"future proofing our house," said Adam—and in part to avoid dramatic increases in premiums. He speculated, "I'm paying $2,000 a year now. . . . It'll probably go up to $10,000 because I've already collected on insurance. They're going to want their money back, right?"[36]

All over the neighborhood, homeowners were transforming their welcoming bungalows into imposing behemoths, set next to homes that still needed to be gutted. It changed the tenor of the community. The residents that had joined together in the face of devastation were now physically separated by daunting flights of stairs rising from the sidewalk to their front doors. Glen Perroth received a letter from his flood insurance broker, warning that if he didn't raise his home, the insurance premium would go up to $9,500 annually. It was more than $9,000 over what he was paying before Sandy. If he went up four feet, the rate would drop to $1,500. Seven feet, $350 each year. What choice did he have?[37] In Keansburg, Sal Cortale said, "you don't have to drive too far, and you'll see a couple houses that are already up . . . and there's three flights of stairs before you get up to the front door." The problem, he said, was that "most of those people [were] seventy [to] eighty years old." Climbing the stairs on a calm day was challenging enough. But in another storm? "It will be interesting to see what happens when emergency squads have to get into some of these houses."[38] For some, the transformations signaled an end of the Bayshore as they knew it—the destructive legacy of a devastating storm. These residents mourned not just the changing landscape but also the loss of the neighborliness that comes from chatting on front stoops and lingering on welcoming street-level porches.

The changes called to mind, too, a loss of Jane Jacobs's "eyes on the street." To preserve the safety of a community, Jacobs wrote in *The Death and Life of Great American Cities* in 1961, "there must be eyes on the street, eyes belonging

**FIGURE 5.1**  In-progress house raising in Keyport. September 28, 2014. Photo by Collette Kennedy.

to those we might call the natural proprietors of the street. The buildings on a street equipped to handle strangers and to ensure the safety of both residents and strangers must be oriented to the street. They cannot turn their backs or blank sides on it and leave it blind."[39] What effect might these elevated houses have on the neighborhood's real—or perceived—safety? Would residents still feel comfortable walking down the street? Would the neighborhood still feel neighborly?

For Bixby, meanwhile, the new federal guidelines meant the potential for growth, even progress. "Fingers crossed," he said, "that some of these renovations that we put into these houses will actually, hopefully, make the property values go up at some point."[40] Because the damage to their home had exceeded 50 percent of its worth, the Bixbys were eligible for FEMA's Increased Cost of Compliance (ICC) coverage, a program designed to defray the costs of mitigating the risk of future damage.[41] The family received $30,000 in ICC coverage, enough to cover the cost of elevation. But, of course, they had to move out again. And this time, FEMA wasn't paying.[42]

For a year, Adam and his wife covered everything out of pocket. The burden was overwhelming. "We're going to be living in this house for the rest of our lives," they thought, "[and] we'll basically be having to pay off all our credit card bills for the rest of our lives, too. . . . It [was] a massive burden put on us."[43] Then they learned about the Rehabilitation, Reconstruction, Elevation, and Mitigation Program (RREM). RREM offered $1.34 billion in federal funds that the state of New Jersey allocated to eligible homeowners to repair or rebuild homes impacted by Sandy. The program was intended as a stopgap, offering residents more than $150,000 to meet needs unfilled by insurance, small-business loans, FEMA, or donations. The paperwork was crushing. There were reports to file, letters to certify, more contractor estimates and engineer appraisals.[44]

For Millie Gonzalez, it was more than just paperwork. Renovating her home to meet both NFIP specifications and the requirements laid out in the Americans with Disabilities Act was nearly impossible. "For every inch you go up," she said, "you need a foot of ramp. If we raise our house forty-eight inches [the minimum required by the new flood-plain regulations for her block] . . . then I need a forty-eight-foot ramp. My property is only fifty by one hundred. My ramp is going to be down the street."[45] Nine months after the storm, Millie was still living with her sister in Keansburg. She had tried to secure temporary housing, but finding something that was both safe and accessible had proven difficult. The accessible housing options she was offered, she said, "were in communities that did not feel safe to me . . . as a woman, as a person with disability, all of it just did not feel safe." She would have felt comfortable being in Union Beach, she said, but nothing was available there. She wanted so desperately to return to the neighborhood she loved. But now with the new NFIP guidelines, she was unsure. "That is the only thing making me reconsider living [there]," she sighed.[46]

For many on the Bayshore, entities like the NFIP and FEMA seemed divorced from the lived experiences and local context of those struggling to rebuild in the aftermath of extreme storms like Sandy. That was not always the case. When James Lee Witt left FEMA in 2001, following the election of George W. Bush, FEMA was one of the most highly regarded agencies in the federal government. Project Impact was launched by FEMA in 1997 in order to support local authorities in natural-hazards preparedness and was credited with mitigating the effects of several disasters in the waning years of the twentieth century. Witt, according to the reporter Mark Murray, had achieved "hero status" in the nation's capital.[47] Policymakers on both sides of the political aisle lauded the director for imbuing the agency with meaning and mission, for placing FEMA at the front lines of disaster response in the United States, and for cutting through bureaucratic holding patterns and allocating resources where they were needed most. Under Witt, FEMA had maintained its all-hazards mission and continued to work toward natural-hazards mitigation and remediation. He had placed FEMA on the front lines of working with communities to assess vulnerabilities created by the interaction between human development and the environment, and he had lent credence to the idea that there was "no such thing as a natural disaster, an acknowledgement," the historian Scott Knowles wrote, that "disaster losses (human and material) reflect the underlying stratification of a society."[48] In short, Witt had made FEMA relevant. "I think the country owes him a debt of gratitude for his service over the last eight years," said Senator Daniel Akaka of Hawaii at the confirmation hearings for Witt's successor, Joe Allbaugh. "No one needs to remind you that you'll be following [the] footsteps of a big man."[49]

Allbaugh was unanimously confirmed under the assumption that he would preserve and protect the model of disaster preparedness that Witt had created.[50] Within his first months in Washington, though, he set about systematically dismantling the programs that Witt and his team had built. First, with the support of the Bush administration, he slashed Project Impact. Then he targeted the agency's postdisaster mitigation programs. Seeking to curtail what he saw as political patronage and wasteful spending, Allbaugh focused FEMA's resources around prehazard planning, with little regard or sympathy for those affected by disasters once they hit. A public relations nightmare occurred in the early months of the Bush administration; the Mississippi River ran over, flooding the town of Davenport, Iowa, for the third time in eight years. Allbaugh tangled with Davenport mayor Phil Yerington, excoriating local politicians and policymakers for their lack of flood-protection measures. "How many times will the American taxpayer have to step in and take care of this flooding, which could be easily prevented by building levees and dikes?" Allbaugh lectured. "There is a point of no return. I don't know whether it's two strikes, you're out—three strikes, you're out. But obviously these homes and properties that are continually flooding, it is not fair to the American taxpayer to ask them time in and time out to pay for rebuilding."[51]

In a public battle that occupied headlines for several days, Allbaugh came across as insensitive and uncaring. The agency director ultimately apologized, but the episode marked a turning point for FEMA's position in Washington and the stellar reputation in natural-hazards mitigation that Witt had worked so hard to build. In the months that followed, Allbaugh—with the support of Vice President Dick Cheney—began the process of shifting the agency's priorities toward counterterrorism.[52]

That was in April 2001. Five months later, in the wake of the September 11, 2001, attacks, FEMA's responses bore close resemblance to those in the days and weeks following the Oklahoma City bombing in 1995. The agency dispatched Urban Search and Rescue teams to comb through collapsed structures and then worked closely with local and state officials in the recovery efforts that followed. Bruce Baughman, a longtime deputy to Witt, served as director of operations, and Allbaugh was pleased with Baughman's leadership and the agency's response in the aftermath of the attacks. But he said in an interview with CNN on October 4, "It's now time to go to the next step into the twenty-first century for all federal agencies, quite frankly, and they need to be thinking about the unthinkable." The time had come, said Allbaugh, for FEMA to shift its full focus toward counterterrorism.[53]

Washington, however, had other ideas. Led by Senator Joseph Lieberman of Connecticut, Congress created a new Department of Homeland Security, designed to be an umbrella organization for all emergency-preparedness measures in the United States, with the director serving in a cabinet position and reporting directly to the president. By the time the new agency became operational in 2003, FEMA had been subsumed under its authority. Over the next two years, as per the recommendations of the 9/11 Commission Report, FEMA's power and resources diminished dramatically. Tom Ridge, the director of homeland security, returned the agency to a civil defense–style model and focused its attention on the increasing threat of terrorism on US soil. Though many favored this new focus, policymakers from urban centers around the nation feared that the federal funding model that followed, allocating resources equally among the states rather than through the previous risk-assessment model that would have prioritized areas with environmental and developmental vulnerabilities, would compromise critical infrastructures in sensitive regions of the country.[54]

In the summer of 2005, the nation saw the disastrous effects of the reorganization. When Hurricane Katrina made landfall in southeastern Louisiana on August 29, the stripping of FEMA's power was laid bare. Katrina tore through the region as a Category 3 storm. It destroyed bridges and roadways, ripped houses from their moorings, crashed through levees and floodwalls, and decimated communities from Houston to Florida. Katrina caused more than 1,200 deaths and over $108 billion in property damage, by far the costliest Atlantic hurricane in the history of the country.[55]

The calamity of Katrina wasn't a surprise. Just a year before the storm hit, a working group comprising representatives from the National Weather Service, the US Army Corps of Engineers, the Louisiana State University Hurricane Center, and various state and federal agencies came together to develop a response strategy in the event of a catastrophic storm striking Louisiana. The group concluded that the hypothetical Hurricane Pam, modeled as the "perfect storm," would bring catastrophic flooding to New Orleans, killing thousands of people and paralyzing the city for several months. "We made great progress this week in our disaster preparedness efforts," said FEMA Regional Director Ron Castleman in a postexercise press release. "Disaster response teams developed action plans in critical areas such as search and rescue, medical care, sheltering, temporary housing, school restoration, and debris management. These plans are essential for quick response to a hurricane but will also help in other emergencies."[56] Following the project, Walter Maestri, the disaster manager for the state's Jefferson Parish, ordered ten thousand body bags—just in case.[57]

Policymakers and city and state officials thought they were ready. What they hadn't prepared for, the sociologist William Freudenberg wrote, "was the stunning absence of federal response. . . . In a country as rich and technologically advanced as the United States—able to deliver astonishing quantities of food and medical supplies, seemingly within a matter of hours, to almost any location on earth—the help somehow failed to arrive within [its] own borders, day after day, even as the agony continued to grow." Although the storm exposed vulnerabilities in the region's urban development and long-term planning, even more striking, Freudenberg continued, was the scope of institutional inattention. It was, he argued, "stunningly systematic, involving all levels of government."[58]

On the Bayshore, residents used Katrina as a touchstone, a benchmark by which to measure their own progress. When relief came, they perceived that the federal government had learned from its mistakes seven years earlier. "I think Sandy was handled a thousand times better than Katrina was," Bixby reflected in 2015. "Katrina was a disaster on multiple levels, from the storm itself all the way down to the government. [Katrina] was just a disaster, whereas [Sandy], for what it was, it was well-handled."[59] But when the recovery stalled, residents came to see the fallout from Katrina as the source of their trouble, believing that they were paying the price for the mistakes of 2005. "I think they [the federal government] learned from Katrina," said Michael Melfi. "They learned a lot of lessons, so they made it a little tougher this time around for people to get their money."[60] Roger Michalak agreed. "What happened with Katrina (so we've heard)," he said, was that "[FEMA] came into New Orleans and they gave people money. Then the people took the money and ran. They didn't throw money back into the towns. . . . So, what FEMA did after that was say, 'Here, we'll give you so much.' But it's not enough. And they didn't give it. If they gave any money out, I would have been on it. It's real sad."[61]

For more than a year after Sandy, Anthony Cavallo made mortgage payments on a house he couldn't live in. "We almost had an apartment," he said. "We were sitting in the apartment and we signed the paperwork, and the guy said, 'We're going for approval.'" Three days later, Cavallo backed out. "I couldn't rent an apartment for $1,800 a month plus utilities and pay a mortgage. I would have gone broke." He could have made it work for a month, maybe two. But for how long their renovations would take? "I would have lost the house."[62]

They collected $2,800 from FEMA for temporary housing. His wife's employer pitched in, too, taking up a collection among her coworkers and drawing from the company's emergency fund. The Cavallos used the money to purchase a two-bedroom trailer, and they parked it in their driveway. They outfitted it with a queen bed for themselves and a twin camping mattress for their daughter, Amy. For the three of them, it was tight. "So cozy," he joked, "that if you step on my foot again, I'm going to kill you." In June, Amy went to visit her grandparents in Cincinnati. The Cavallos drove out to drop her off, and on the way, they stopped for a night at a hotel. "Me and my wife got into bed that night and we just smiled and looked at each other."[63] After nine months, they finally got to sleep in a real bed.

It felt like a turning point, the start of a new beginning. And then, said Cavallo, "FEMA backed out on us."[64] The agency had been using federal resources to tear down homes in Union Beach. The Cavallos had postponed demolition several times, in a holding pattern as the insurance company sorted through the erosion question. "I didn't have the faith," Anthony lamented. "I had the faith in God that I should have gone with it, but I didn't have the faith in the insurance company that if I took this down, I [would have] enough money to build a house." If his claim weren't resolved, he wouldn't have the funds for a complete renovation. Without some kind of assurance, he couldn't risk tearing it down.[65]

Finally, they were on the list for summer demolition. "And just as they were about to start," he said, "FEMA said, 'We've changed the rules. Unless the house is in imminent danger of collapse, we're not paying to take it down.' So, now the homeowners have to pay."[66] In the first nine months after Sandy, FEMA had demolished 170 homes in Union Beach. According to borough officials, the agency pulled funding for 84 of the remaining 92 properties. At least 50 of those that remained required asbestos remediation. "They're all dangerous to live in," Union Beach administrator Jennifer Maier told the local CBS news affiliate. "But I can't prove that they're going to fall down tomorrow. So, because I can't prove that, they refuse to pay."[67] In response, a spokesperson for FEMA called attention to the agency's Demolition of Private Structures policy, which states that funding for demolition is predicated on "certification that homes to be demolished are in imminent danger of full or partial collapse." Only 8 of the remaining homes on the list for Union Beach met that standard, FEMA said.[68]

The Cavallos benefited from a volunteer construction crew, who came in with cranes to flatten the house. But they had to pay for removal. "Disposing of material is expensive," said Anthony. "So, now we have to use the homeowner's [policy] to pay for that." They were borrowing from Peter to pay Paul. "We have to use the insurance money to have our house taken down, which is more money that's coming out of the new house. . . . You've got to keep scaling back, and scaling back, and scaling back."[69]

Residents were angry. "This is a middle-class area," said Port Monmouth's John Piasecki. John and his wife, Maureen, had to replace their heating and electrical system after the storm. Their yard was ruined, as was the entire contents of their garage and basement. They considered themselves among the lucky ones. Their house was one of only two on their block with the first floor still intact.[70] "We're working people," he said. "We don't have money to pay $15,000 a year for flood insurance, or money to elevate the houses. So, if this is what they're going to demand people to do, then they're going to need to come up with some cash for people to do it."[71]

For Mary Jane and Roger Michalak, it was a devastating blow. "We don't know what to do," Mary Jane told reporters when the decision was announced. "They took down every house on the beach front," Roger said, "and they can't seem to do the same for all the residents?"[72] Like the Cavallos, the Michalaks had been living in a two-bedroom trailer in their driveway. They had felt fortunate, right after the storm, to connect with a helpful FEMA agent. "Because we didn't have a computer," Mary Jane said. "They put everything into the computer and helped us with our rent. A lot of people don't know how to do that."[73] Still, their new quarters were cramped. To escape, they spent their days volunteering at the borough's Hurricane Sandy Help Center. Before the storm, the space had housed a senior center. Mary Jane had been the president. "And then the first day of the storm," she said, "they wanted to open things up. . . . We opened the doors, and we've been here ever since. Every day."[74] They put out donuts, served coffee—"a million cups of cups of coffee, already"—answered questions, and chatted with weary residents. They looked on as their friends packed up and left. For some, it was just too expensive to rebuild. Roger said, "This week, it was like a farewell party because people were coming and saying goodbye. . . . They can't rebuild with what they're given. It's not the people. The people want to stay. It's the insurance company, and the banking industry. The entire structure."[75]

A year after they applied for federal relief, and two years after Sandy, the Bixby family got good news. They had been approved for a RREM grant; they would receive enough to reimburse them for all of their out-of-pocket expenses.[76] For others, the relief never came. The Michalaks ended up paying out of pocket to get the asbestos in their home removed. In October 2014, their house finally came down. But the financial hits kept coming. "I still have to pay my sewer bill. I still have to pay my taxes. Even though I don't have a house, I still have to pay my taxes until August of 2014. . . . I'm not paying on my land. I'm paying on something I don't even have on my land."[77]

A year later, the Michalaks were still living in the trailer, parked in a driveway that dead-ended at an empty lot. "People who had insurance didn't get taken care of," said Roger. "I just pray to God," Mary Jane pled, "that they'll call, and us get into a house before we die."[78] On the two-year anniversary of the storm, there were still 128 empty lots in Union Beach. Of the 298 homes that had been destroyed in the borough, less than 60 percent had been rebuilt.[79] "Everybody says, 'when this is done, you should take [your trailer] and put it in Pennsylvania as a weekend home,'" Cavallo said. "When we're done with this, I don't ever want to see the thing again. I'll burn it . . . I never want to sleep in a trailer a day in my life after this."[80]

# "THERE IS NO SUCH THING AS A NATURAL DISASTER"

At 7:00 p.m. on March 21, 2013, Middletown residents gathered for an update on the Port Monmouth Flood Project. It had been thirteen years since the project first began, thirteen years since, under the Water Resources Development Act of 2000, the Army Corps of Engineers undertook a study of the Raritan and Sandy Hook Bays designed to "reduce storm and tide induced flooding at the community of Port Monmouth, NJ."[1] Based on the study's findings, the act authorized the construction of levees, floodwalls, dunes, beach fill, storm gates, and other closure structures—in short, it apportioned funds to protect the Bayshore from flooding. The money was there, allocated in the federal budget at the turn of the twenty-first century. It never arrived.

It was a packed house at Veterans of Foreign Wars (VFW) Post 2179 on Highway 36. Iris Miranda was there. So were Adam Bixby, Bob Pulsch, the Melfis, and the Piaseckis.[2] They were there because their lives had been turned upside down five months earlier, and they wanted to know why. Frustrated residents bombarded local and state officials with accusations. Why did the project stall out? What had happened to the funds? Could Sandy's destruction have been avoided?

The question of environmental readiness haunted Bayshore residents in the months after Sandy made landfall. It wasn't the immediate preparations that concerned them. "They had mandatory evacuations," John Piasecki later recalled.[3] The problem was that people didn't leave. "It was a one-time event," Michael Melfi said, something "that's never happened before."[4] Joann agreed. "I think they did the best they could."[5] On one level, they said, there was no way to prepare for this kind of storm. "[It was] a freak occurrence," Pulsch said. "There's no question about it. . . . All the stars were lined up. It just came in."[6] It was the right time and the right place, said Michael Melfi. "I saw a show on National Geographic about the worst-case scenario—what would happen in the New York–New Jersey corridor if a hurricane ever hit it at the right time, and that's exactly what happened."[7] But what about the months before Sandy hit? The years before the storm landfall? What could municipal, state, and federal governments have done to mitigate the damage? And, Bayshore residents wanted to know, why hadn't they done it?

"Help Port Monmouth get back to normal." That's what organizers were calling for at the March 21 meeting. It was a simple plea. "We are asking for the community to join us . . . to sign a petition to release these funds and get Port Monmouth back on the road to recovery and lessen the threat of flooding."[8] But the meeting was mired in data. Attendees couldn't keep up with the steady stream of dates, financial projections, and mitigation analyses that local and state politicians quoted.

For most Bayshore residents, the details of the original flood project from 2000 proved hazy, with conflicting dates and conflated details. "Our neighborhood was scheduled to be done many years ago," said Glen Perroth, "and that money went somewhere else when there was another flood. . ., down in Florida or whatever."[9] It should have started in the early 1990s, said Iris Miranda. "From what I understand, they were supposed to put dunes . . . right here where the Spy House is. They were supposed to put a floodgate over there [by the marina]."[10] She recalled plans for a floodgate at the fishery on Main Street and drains in the wetlands. "We've had a flood wall plan, a flood control system plan, approved by the Army Corps of Engineers, I think in 1997 or 2000," said Anthony Cavallo. "This was approved many, many years ago, all set to go. The federal government never funded the project. Had the federal government funded this flood control wall system fifteen years ago or so, maybe this [wouldn't have] happen[ed]."[11] Thirteen years ago, said John Piasecki, "the federal government had allocated $30 million for the project. By 2013, the necessary funds had ballooned to $91 million."[12] Still, the overall takeaway was the same: "They knew it was going to happen," said Miranda. "The storm was waiting."[13] And, said Pulsch, "they weren't prepared."[14]

In 2012, Hurricane Sandy was considered a 1 percent storm. That is, in any given year, there was a 1 percent chance that a storm causing that magnitude of damage would hit the New Jersey coastline. By 2050, said David Kutner, planning manager at New Jersey Future, the chance of such a storm occurring in any given year will increase to 10 percent.[15] The reason for the increase is two-fold, according to Kutner. First, Americans are flocking to the coast. In 1970, 88.5 million Americans lived along the nation's coastlines. Over the next forty years that number increased by 34.8 million, such that in 2010, 39 percent of the US population was living in coastal counties that accounted for less than 10 percent of the nation's total land area (excluding Alaska). By 2020, those numbers were expected to increase to upward of 134 million: an 8 percent rise in the span of a decade.[16] "Our population," said Kutner, "has been gravitating toward areas of the United States for settlement that scientists are repeatedly and continuously, at much greater rates, telling us are at tremendous risk."[17] This threat, Scott Knowles wrote, lies at the center of modern urban history in the US. It is a history, he argued, "of risk-taking and unsustainable development."[18]

Second, sea levels are rising at unprecedented rates, magnifying the risks posed by mounting development. Sea-level rise was first linked to climate concerns in 1965. In November of that year, the President's Science Advisory Committee presented Lyndon Johnson with a report, authored by thirty esteemed scientists from around the nation, outlining several possible effects of the increased atmospheric carbon dioxide that the atmospheric scientist Charles David Keeling had observed over the previous several years. In "Restoring the Quality of Our Environment," the advisory committee warned that this higher concentration of gases would cause dire environmental consequences. These atmospheric shifts would cause a gradual but significant warming of the planet, they wrote, which could lead to melting of the Antarctic ice cap, warming sea water, and rising sea levels. "Through his worldwide industrial civilization," the authors concluded, "man is unwittingly conducting a vast geographic experiment. Within a few generations he is burning the fossil fuels that slowly accumulated over the past 500 million years. By the year 2000 the increase in atmospheric $CO_2$ will be close to 25 percent. This may be sufficient to produce measurable and perhaps marked changes in climate and will almost certainly cause changes in the temperature and other properties of the atmosphere."[19] The earth, they warned, was experiencing atmospheric and oceanic changes at unprecedented rates.

By the turn of the twenty-first century, these concerns were no longer hypothetical. Temperatures were climbing; arctic snow and ice cover was shrinking; atmospheric water vapor was increasing; seas were rising. The Third National Climate Change Assessment, released in 2014, painted a dire picture. "Worldwide," the report read, "the observed changes in average conditions have been accompanied by increasing trends in extremes of heat and heavy precipitation events and decreases in extreme cold. It is the sum total of these indicators that leads to the conclusion that warming of our planet is unequivocal."[20] That same year, the Union of Concerned Scientists warned, "Sea level along the mid-Atlantic coast is now rising more than three times the global pace—partly because the land is sinking. Over the past one hundred years, sea level has risen more than fifteen inches at Atlantic City."[21] The consequences were significant, especially for

New Jersey. "Today," said Kutner in 2015, "any of those communities experiencing regular flooding are expected, by 2050, to experience it at a much greater rate. They need to change their development patterns to address it. It's not enough just to take your car and move it away from the beach for a little while."[22]

These patterns of development brought the story of Sandy into sharp focus. As beachfront construction proliferated, it stripped away the natural barriers that protected against coastal storms. In 1962, the Ash Wednesday storm, then considered the worst storm ever to hit New Jersey, carved three new channels through Long Beach Island into the Barnegat Bay, forever reshaping the Atlantic coastline and prompting statewide initiatives geared toward replenishment and shore protection. Following the historic nor'easter, the state legislature earmarked $25 million annually toward fortifying the coast, setting off a chain of events that, by the turn of the twenty-first century, saw New Jersey receiving a higher percentage of federal aid reserved for storm protection than any other state in the nation. But these initiatives proved inadequate amidst the ongoing beachfront development.[23] Seven months before Hurricane Sandy began gathering energy in the Atlantic Ocean, as the state commemorated the fiftieth anniversary of the Ash Wednesday storm, the New Jersey climatologist David Robinson warned, "Replenishment might help, but it's barely a band-aid when a storm pounds away at the coastal defenses. Everything is vulnerable. It's not as if these storms come with any cyclicity or regularity. They've come before. They're going to come again."[24]

Shoreline development compounded the effects of the state's rising sea levels about which Kutner warned. In Little Egg Harbor, just north of the New Jersey's Great Bay on the southern Atlantic coast, those sea-level rise projections indicate that in 2050, the relative land impact of a 1 percent storm would be roughly 8 percent greater than in 2010. "But the number of parcels [on the shoreline]," said Kutner, "increases by fourfold. . . . The depth of the water creates the impact, so under 2050 sea-level rise, the water [in normal conditions] doesn't quite come up to the level of the houses in a lot of the areas of the town." But when a storm of Sandy's magnitude hits the coast? "It completely covers them."[25]

Sandy "has brought [climate change] into focus," Sister Sharon Kelly of the Bayshore Community Center said, "at least for those of us who have suffered. . . . I think the reality is that we're all going to have to deal with how we prepare for this changing climate." Kelly continued, "I hope it's made our officials and our society a little bit more aware that we can't control nature," referencing the mansions along the barrier islands on the Long Island Sound and the need for shoreline restoration and beachfront protection in place of continued development.[26] Andrea Bulvid and James Butler assessed that vulnerability similarly. "I think this needs to be a big lesson in protecting the wetlands," Bulvid said. "Because water has to go someplace."[27] Butler believed his community was increasingly vulnerable. "We lost a lot of sand. We lost a lot of protection." But he cautioned, "It's not just that we need some kind of protection on the beach, but also the right protection."[28]

Although long-term municipal planning alone will not diminish the ferocity of storms, mitigation efforts like those Butler and Bulvid offered and like those proposed for Port Monmouth in 2000—or the absence thereof—serve as critical predictors of property destruction during coastal storms.[29] Hurricane Katrina made this clear in 2005. Before the storm made landfall, New Orleans had long been the focus of hurricane experts and disaster managers. The coastal city, which juts out across the brackish estuary known as Lake Pontchartrain and sits largely below sea level, was widely regarded as one of the most vulnerable urban spaces in the nation.[30]

Perhaps nothing played a greater role in escalating New Orleans's vulnerability to storm damage than the degradation of the region's protected wetlands in the preceding forty years, most notably because of the construction of the Mississippi River–Gulf Outlet (MRGO) Canal, a seventy-six-mile manmade shipping channel that runs parallel to the Mississippi River. The project was authorized by the Rivers and Harbors Act of 1956; the Army Corps of Engineers completed construction in 1965. The canal was successful in creating a shortcut between the Gulf of Mexico and the city's inner harbor, but it had the unintended effect of vastly accelerating the disappearance of the surrounding wetlands. By decade's end, Louisiana was losing approximately forty-five square miles of coastal wetlands each year. Thirty years later, more than 20 percent of the state's wetlands had vanished—roughly the same amount that the Mississippi River had built up in the previous thousand years. William Freudenberg wrote, "It would be difficult to imagine another threat to the wetlands more significant than the MRGO."[31]

The canal caused dramatic shifts in the ecosystem of coastal Louisiana. The lack of natural current meant that saltwater slowly meandered up the MRGO, decimating a once robust cypress tree population. With the strong cypress roots no longer supporting the marshy soil, silt and mud built up along the channel floor, requiring routine dredging, which had the effect of widening the channel with each subsequent year. When Hurricane Katrina hit, forty years after the canal's completion, the section closest to New Orleans was roughly half a mile wide.[32] The wider channel meant that more water could rush through at substantially higher speeds.

On August 29, 2005, as Katrina churned through the Gulf, the storm surge swept up the estuary with such force that it caused three separate ruptures in New Orleans's floodwalls. As the *Washington Post* reported two months later, the breaks in the walls along Lake Pontchartrain unleashed "a wall of water that swept entire buildings from their foundations and transformed what might have been a routine hurricane into the costliest storm in US history."[33] These breaks, suggested the *Post*, were not the result of environmental forces but rather "design flaws." According to investigators, the soil beneath the walls had been substantially weakened before the storm. It was the same story insurance adjusters told Cavallo three weeks after Sandy; the damage to his home had been caused by erosion of the soil beneath his foundation. The vulnerability meant that when the foundation became saturated—for Cavallo's house during Sandy and for the floodwalls of Lake Pontchartrain during Katrina—it began to slide. Adding to that, the investigators concluded, the MRGO—that "little-used navigation canal"—was responsible for "amplifying and intensifying" Katrina's initial surge, "contributing to a third floodwall collapse."[34] Knowles noted two lessons to draw from Katrina: "First, the city and water are not separate. Second, separating them insults history, and, if the past is ignored, eventually you will find yourself marooned on a rooftop in a sea of survivors who can't connect."[35]

Critics in New Jersey could not directly point to any one project that magnified the impact of Hurricane Sandy along the New Jersey coastline the way MRGO did along the Gulf Coast. Instead, the historian Neil Maher wrote, New Jersey suffers from a sort of "ecological schizophrenia."[36] The environmental history of the state is at once a story of industrial growth and shoreline development and one of vast green space and fierce coastal protection.

During the first half of the twentieth century, in the Garden State and around the country, land management policies adhered to federal regulations prioritizing commercial development over wetland protection. The 1962 Ash Wednesday storm and the environmental consciousness that began to emerge from it prompted growing criticism of such policies. But the effects of that longstanding development were already becoming clear. As the historians Heather Fenyk and David H. Guston wrote, "While residents of many New Jersey communities looked from their windows and witnessed tracts of open space disappearing rapidly, they also experienced more tangible troubles from rivers and streams that flooded main streets and basements. Feeling that something was drastically wrong, some citizens began tentatively to connect these phenomena."[37]

In the years that followed, local campaigns coalesced into successful statewide and nationwide lobbying efforts, agitating for greater environmental safeguards. In 1977, the federal Clean Water Act offered the first nationwide wetlands protection program. In New Jersey, the Wetland Act of 1970 and the 1987 Freshwater Wetlands Protection Act (FWPA) created protections for saltwater and freshwater wetlands across the state, positioning New Jersey's policies among the most progressive in the nation. Fenyk and Guston praised then governor Thomas Kean for his "courageous" decision, in 1987, to issue a moratorium on wetlands construction during legislative hearings for the FWPA.[38]

Kean's climate initiatives and subsequent state-level policies earned New Jersey the reputation as a leader in national environmental protection efforts over the next quarter century. In 2007, the state created the Blue Acres Program, through which the government could purchase flood-prone properties and reclaim the land for recreation and conservation. At its inception, the Green Acres, Water Supply and Floodplain Protection, and Farmland and Historic Preservation Bond Act of 2007 authorized $12 million for the program. Two years later, a comparable 2009 act allocated an additional $24 million.[39]

When Chris Christie took office in January 2010, his environmental agenda put him at odds with the longstanding priorities of the state legislature. In 2011, seventeen months before Sandy hit, the governor announced that the New Jersey would be withdrawing from the Regional Greenhouse Gas Initiative, a comprehensive interstate plan to reduce the area's carbon footprint by limiting carbon dioxide emissions from power plants and creating cap-and-trade limitations on permits for utility companies.[40] Christie's action marked a striking reversal in state policy dating back to the 1970 Wetlands Act.

Even as the governor's political clout soared in the months following Sandy—thirteen months after the storm, he won re-election by a margin of 28.1 percent—in the years that followed, climate activists condemned the governor for his apparent rejection of environmental priorities. In January 2014, Ben Adler of *Grist*, an online publication focusing on environmental coverage, took Christie to task for his record on climate change. "Look up anything about recovery from Superstorm Sandy on official New Jersey government websites," wrote Adler, "and you might notice something odd." On the web page for New Jersey's Office of Recovery and Rebuilding, "mitigation," "resilience," and "flood," appeared a total of forty-seven times.[41] Meanwhile, the words "climate," "sea," "ocean," or "rise/rising" were absent. Adler found that in press releases, Christie noted his "commitment to a strong and resilient shore," without, said Adler, mentioning "why the shore is imperiled in the first place." Adler saw no mention of climate change or sea-level rise in the New Jersey Department of Environmental Protection's public communications, nor in an action plan for disaster-recovery block grants from the state Department of Community Affairs. Even the Blue Acres Frequently Asked Questions webpage, noted Adler, avoided any mention of sea-level rise in its description of the values of the program, instead offering the vague claim, "An important benefit is that your family will be safe and out of harm's way."[42]

Six months after the publication of the *Grist* article, when the governor announced new regulations on coastal construction—the first since Sandy—critics once again charged the administration with ignoring any potential lessons from the storm. The proposal, which created automated processes for building permits, eased previous regulations on coastline development. Representatives from the administration offered that the proposal was meant to encourage rebuilding and stimulate the state's economy and tourism infrastructure.[43]

The editorial board at the *Star Ledger*, the largest newspaper in New Jersey, took the governor to task. "You'd think the Christie administration's first major overhaul of rules regulating coastal construction since Hurricane Sandy would focus on lessons learned," the board wrote on June 29, 2014, "and how we can better protect ourselves against future storm. But no. Believe it or not, its new policies ignore the science of sea level rise and all dire warnings and new studies about climate change in the nearly two years since the storm hit."[44] They chronicled criticisms to the proposal from environmental groups across the state and documented the limitations to current regulations that New Jerseyans mistakenly expected the new plan to address. "Sandy showed us the folly of building up along the water's edge," the board concluded. "It's so simple it shouldn't need to be said: why create new governmental policies that put more people's lives and property at risk?"[45] In a 2018 interview with the *Huffington Post*, Jeff Tittel, director of the New Jersey chapter of the Sierra Club, said, "Christie's legacy will be trying to roll back every other governor's environmental legacy. He's been the most anti-environmental governor this state has ever seen."[46]

Despite the national repudiation of Christie's environmental policies, for many of the working-class homeowners of Port Monmouth, Union Beach, Keyport, and Keansburg, green initiatives were complicated, especially in the midst of the ongoing recovery from Sandy. The storm had brought into sharp relief the need for shoreline protection. They wanted to see structural remedies like berms, levies, and sandbars. They wanted wetland protection. But broader policies of climate action felt removed from their everyday reality. For some, environmentalism was a luxury, an elite club that required disposable income to join.[47] Increased taxes on production meant that it cost more to buy food, to drive a car, and to purchase material goods, and these burdens disproportionately affected lower-income communities. In a May 2013 interview with NBC correspondent Matt Lauer, Christie played on this notion of exclusivity. "I haven't been shown any definitive proof yet that that's what caused [Hurricane Sandy]," he said. "And this . . . is a distraction. I've got a place to rebuild here and people want to talk to me about esoteric theories."[48] The governor's response, seven months after the storm, seemed to affirm the governor's commitment to the people of New Jersey, still reeling from the storm's devastation.

But there was more to Christie's response to Lauer than an apparent rejection of the dangers of sea-level rise. His statements reflected state-level policies that privileged economic recovery and tourism rebuilding over environmental preparedness, policies which had profound implications for Bayshore residents. Before long, these homeowners—living in a reliably red part of the blue Garden State—began to turn away from the governor and question his professed loyalty to the residents of New Jersey.

Christie made his priorities clear less than a month after the storm. On November 18, 2012, he released early projections for the overall costs of the Sandy cleanup. The number, $29.4 billion, included personal and commercial property damage and loss to transportation infrastructure, utilities, and public works. In his statement that day, the governor pledged specific support to the Jersey shore and its $19 billion in revenue—half of the state's total tourism industry. "We will continue," Christie promised, "to provide immediate relief for our citizens who were struck hard by Sandy. But be assured. I will spare no effort and waste no time to rebuild and restore our tourism industry."[49]

Earlier that week, the Atlantic City Alliance had run its first post-Sandy tourism advertisement. The Do Anything, Do Everything, Do AC campaign included television and radio spots, a national ad in the *New York Times*—the first of its kind for the shore town—and several events around the region, including a sponsored balloon at Philadelphia's Thanksgiving Day Parade. In a press release for the campaign, the alliance noted, "the famed Atlantic City Boardwalk . . . is still intact and as beautiful as ever. The campaign seeks to promote AC as 'open for business' while being sensitive that nearby towns along New Jersey's shoreline sustained serious and long-term damage."[50]

The scope of the state's tourism recovery efforts was expansive. It included op-eds, celebrity telethons, even a special "Restore the Shore" episode of MTV's popular reality show *Jersey Shore*. Just days after Sandy made landfall, Larry Olmsted, contributor to *Forbes*, wrote, "All twelve of Atlantic City's waterfront casinos emerged largely unharmed from the storm and are ready to open as early as the next few days. There is now legalized gambling in almost every corner of the country, and lots of people travel for gaming—maybe your next roll of the dice should be in the spot that needs it most."[51] Olmsted's piece painted an optimistic picture of the post-Sandy shoreline, promising minimal impact to the visitor experience.

Overall, the campaign worked. The state saw tourism revenue rebound by the summer of 2014. Most of the boardwalks were rebuilt by three years after the storm. In 2016, less than three years following the storm, the tourism industry brought in $44.1 billion, up more than $6 billion since Sandy. In May 2017, Seaside Heights' Hydrus roller coaster, replacing the Jet Star coaster that was famously swept into the Atlantic Ocean during the storm and became one of the most iconic and enduring images of Sandy, opened to the public.[52]

Meanwhile, at the VFW in Port Monmouth, neighbors were growing restless. They were tired of numbers. They wanted answers; they wanted someone to blame. Why wasn't there a coordinated mitigation plan across the Bayshore? "If Union Beach had a great flood protection plan," said James Butler, "all we do is push water to Keansburg and Keyport."[53] If the Keansburg floodgates worked, Port Monmouth would get swamped. "Many years ago," said Glen Perroth, "the Keansburg side of the dike was flooding out all the time. It was a regular thing.... So, they put this big mound of dirt all the way down the waterway." They put a floodgate at the end, he continued, "and they close the water trenches before every storm. What happened this time is, the water came up so high, had they not done all that years ago, Keansburg would have gotten all the flooding and we would have been spared." But he acknowledged, "Or maybe everybody would have gotten wet."[54] These were conversations that had vexed the Bayshore for decades. "It's something that always got stalled out and put on the backburner," said Butler. "And we paid the price for that."[55]

In Port Monmouth, these questions of mitigation became amplified both geographically and socioeconomically. Route 36—where the VFW meeting took place—ran parallel to the shoreline east to west and had long served as a de facto dividing line between the wet side of town and the dry side. North of the thoroughfare, you were in the flood plain; south, you could expect a modicum of protection. After the storm, members of the Perroth family stayed with friends on the dry side, just around the corner from their house but sheltered from the violent surges that had destroyed so many properties on the coast.[56] Bulvid took the characterization a step further. "We're technically on the poor side," she said, referencing the area north of Route 36. "I don't really think there is too much different [between the two], except for the price of drugs."[57]

Bulvid's quip was perhaps more perceptive than she realized; in evaluating the human toll of natural hazards, money did matter. Knowles wrote, "Almost invariably, marginalized groups live in more risk-prone geographies, and by definition have fewer resources with which to confront loss. . . . 'There is no such thing as a natural disaster!' has in fact emerged as a critique of power, invoked not only by quiet researchers, but also more powerfully by vocal activists adding 'disaster justice' to similar calls for environmental justice and worker's rights."[58] During Katrina, this so-called vulnerability paradigm—the understanding that structural and economic forces make certain groups more susceptible to damage during disasters—was exposed not only in the long-term urban planning and mitigation efforts but in the acute emergency preparations as well. Those who could afford it left before the storm made landfall. Those who stayed largely represented populations that did not have the means or physical capacity to leave—and then lacked the resources to rebuild. "Hurricane Katrina," Knowles argued, "exposed vulnerabilities rooted in the region's deep historical traditions of racial segregation, economic disadvantage, and environmental risk built into the land in the form of an inadequate levee system."[59] During and after Sandy, said Darlene Finch, mid-Atlantic Regional Coordinator at NOAA's Coastal Services Center, "anecdotal data indicate[d] that the rich [were] okay, and the really poor . . . left, and . . . the blue-collar communities . . . were hit the hardest."[60] The experiences of the residents of Port Monmouth, Keansburg, Keyport, and Union Beach bore that out.

After Sandy, many Bayshore homeowners faced uncertain economic futures. As they contemplated what came next, they knew that they needed to plan with the power of the natural world in mind. "As tough as we think we are or as modern as we are, there are things we can't control," said Sister Kelly.[61] Their frustration during the meeting at the Port Monmouth VFW had given way to thoughtful reflection. "The next version of Union Beach, Union Beach 2.0 that we're building now, will be taller and stronger," said James Butler, "and a little bit kinder to the environment. . . . If you've got enough wetlands, it can absorb some of the water, some waves, before it gets to homeowners. . . . Maybe it's time to look at this town and say, there are areas where you have to give back to the environment, turn it over to Mother Nature, and just use it as a buffer, and we'll head to higher ground."[62]

# EPILOGUE

## New Jersey Strong

On May 29, 2018, Collette Kennedy stood among friends and neighbors at Keyport's Old Glory Kitchen and Spirits to launch her campaign for mayor. She had printed posters for the event: "Keyport Progress—Keyport Pride." Her competitor was Harry Aumack II, an octogenarian whose roots in the town were six generations deep. He was a member of the local volunteer fire department, still driving the truck on area calls. Aumack and Kennedy were friends. The previous month, she had attended his eightieth birthday bash (much to the dismay, she noted, of some of the older Keyport residents, who couldn't understand a friendship between political rivals).

Kennedy was modest in her description of her mayoral bid. Keyport operated under a weak-mayor system, she explained, in which the mayor only votes if the borough council ends up in a tie. "It's not a powerful position in terms of voting on town issues," she demurred. Still, it opened up opportunities that serving on the council—a position she had held since January 1, 2017—precluded. "Where are we with preventative measures for FEMA? What's the status of the new flood maps? These are questions and conversations that can take place with the title of mayor."[1]

Six years earlier, if you had asked Kennedy about running for office, she would have balked. She had no intention of entering politics, "absolutely, positively none," she quipped. "I didn't even really understand local government."[2] And then Sandy hit. She spent the next two weeks working the night shift at the Central School emergency shelter, and the next five months running a donation center out of her garage.[3] It started there, she said: "That's how I met people in town that I never would have met otherwise. From there, I joined the local emergency response team, and then became a team leader. I started serving on various committees in town. On January 1, [2013], I was appointed to the environmental commission."[4] It kept building: "I started attending local meetings, because there were so many others in town who were tied up in the recovery, or with their families. I went to FEMA seminars, in Keyport and around the area, to hear what that process was. It was all new to me, because none of that happened after Irene." She enrolled in classes at Kean University, where she worked as an administrative assistant, to pursue a master's degree in public administration. At first, she intended to focus on emergency disaster management, but when a faculty retirement removed those courses from the offerings, she signed up for classes in local governance and found that she enjoyed learning about the inner workings of municipal structures and policies. What came next was a four-year sprint toward her degree. When she finished, she paused. "I needed to do some soul searching," she said, "to figure out what I should do next." She briefly considered a career in homeland security or federal disaster preparedness. But then she turned inward. She reflected on the town she had called home since October 2012, on all the people she had met and all the connections she had made. "Most people, when they go home at night, they go home to take care of their families and their children," she said. "But for me, Keyport is like my family . . . I decided I wasn't done serving this town yet."[5]

In the spring of 2016, Kennedy launched her first campaign for elected office, running for a seat on the Keyport Borough Council. That April, she turned to Facebook—where else?—to announce her candidacy. In doing so, she brought up Sandy and the impact the storm had had on the community:

> This past week marked 3 & 1/2 years since Hurricane Sandy—the storm and its aftermath brought extreme challenges to our local residents and businesses. It also brought out great volunteer groups and fundraising ideas and projects for people to unite for the cause. So many people didn't just talk the talk they showed that actions speak louder than words. As a reminder that some things take time and even though not all of the projects and homes are complete yet I went through some photos from some of the projects since the storm to show that the teamwork many people displayed is something I will never forget. Together Everyone Achieves More. I am grateful that I was able to be able to assist with so many of the projects and still continue to today and will do so until everyone in our area is back home. #humanityprevails[6]

As life-changing as Sandy was for Kennedy herself, it was equally transformative for the borough of Keyport, a town long stymied in entrenched infighting and parochial protocols and policies. Sandy showed residents the possibilities that can come from putting politics aside. "Everyone working together at the shelter," said Kennedy, "there were no politics in that. . . . When you look at the monumental task that was ahead of us, and how we did it, you see that people can work together."[7]

By 2018, Keyport was moving forward collaboratively. "Our town is in a really good place right now," said Kennedy, not hiding her pride in the strides Keyport had made. "We're working together. Regardless of the outcome of the election, I feel like I'm winning because we're all getting along."[8] The borough was attracting new homebuyers, families from New York in search of a more affordable commuter suburb. On average, properties only lasted three days on the market before being bought up. Realtors in adjacent neighborhoods were relying on the Keyport zip code to boost interest. In 2016, there were twenty-two empty storefronts downtown. Two years later, that number was down to only a few. Some of these changes, no doubt, stem from Keyport's relative protection from the storm; the town incurred less catastrophic damage during Sandy than neighboring Union Beach and Cliffwood. But Sandy had also changed the culture of the community.[9]

Not all Bayshore towns were so fortunate. Five years after the storm, a tour of Union Beach revealed rows of boarded-up properties and dozens of trailers, still parked in the driveways of uninhabitable homes. On some blocks, ornate houses loomed high above street-level, casting shadows over abandoned bungalows, the infamous orange stickers still affixed to the front door. In some ways, the town felt stuck in time, the rebuilding process halting and uneven. It was easy to imagine Roger and Mary Jane Michalak still sharing the buy-one-get-one special at McDonald's because their insurance payout—supposedly a $250,000 policy—didn't end up covering the cost of a new car.[10]

Still, there were signs of progress. After nearly five years, Jakeabob's was finally getting ready to open its doors for the 2017 season, albeit without indoor seating. The recovery was taxing for Gigi Dorr, the restaurant's owner. She wished that there had been a manual for how to rebuild. "We needed a binder," she said, someone, or something, to tell her exactly what to do when the next storm hits. "That's what was missing here." After a lengthy—and losing—battle with her insurance company, in 2014 she was awarded a $2 million loan from the state's Economic Development Authority. It was enough to reopen the Union Beach staple at its original capacity. Still, Dorr felt cautious. She needed to know that the beaches were secure, that the Army Corps of Engineers protection project would work. She needed to believe that the investment—emotional as much as financial—would be worth it. So she started with the tiki bar. And people came—in droves. On warm, sunny days, they filled every seat. It almost felt like life before

Sandy. But there was no protection from the elements without operable indoor seating. And when the air chilled or rain fell, Gigi was forced to close for the day. In the first month of the 2018 season, they shut their doors four times. It wasn't perfect. But they were moving forward.[11]

The Hope Tree still lived at the corner of Jersey Avenue and Shore Road. James Butler—Mr. Hope Tree—saw the tree as a symbol of the Union Beach's own Sandy story, a story, said Butler, "of resilience. . . . Bad things absolutely do happen to good people, and there is suffering, and things are going to happen in your life that you will not like. But the rest of your life is defined by your response to that." Union Beach, he implied, responded with hope. Butler summed it up well. "*Strong* won't get you anywhere. *Tough* won't get you anywhere. You better figure out how to be smart, and you better figure out how to have some kind of hope to hold on to. Otherwise, they make it really easy to just give up and throw in the towel."[12] People started referring to the town as Union Beach 2.0. "Mr. Hope Tree came up with that," said Anthony Cavallo. They even had t-shirts made.[13]

This reclamation of the town brought with it a new set of priorities for residents, as well. "I'm learning to live in the present," Cavallo explained, "not the past. And the future. I'm learning to live in the future, for my daughter." Two years after Sandy, the Cavallos finally moved into their new home. And they were savoring every moment there. "This new house," he reflected, "is going to be geared toward family, entertainment, and God. It's not going to be a place where we come home at the end of the night and turn the TV on for an hour and eat dinner and go to bed. This is going to be a place we're going to enjoy. . ., a place that we're going to have friends over on the weekends, and we're going to have barbecues." For Cavallo, his new house represented a new chance to create the life he wanted to live. "We've got to do it right," he cautioned, "because we're writing our children's and grandchildren's history books."[14]

And the community was seeing cautious progress in its agitation for coastal protections. In Port Monmouth, the Army Corps of Engineers finally commenced a local flood control project in June 2014, fifteen months after that contentious meeting at the local VFW. The first phase of the project, completed twelve months later, focused on wetlands mitigation, creating 15-foot dunes and replenishing the sand along the half-mile shoreline. To make room for the more robust beaches, the project called for a 195-foot extension of the existing fishing pier. The second phase, which got underway in October 2016 and was projected to be completed in 2022, saw the installation of a mile-long concrete floodwall and levee system.[15]

"It used to be a little rinky-dink ten-yard beach," Adam Bixby said. "We'd go down there just to show people that we had a beach. But now, it's awesome. . . . We have a beautiful beach."[16] In August 2020, Hurricane Isaias brought eighty-five mile-per-hour winds to Port Monmouth, testing the new system. "The . . . tide gates and pump stations allowed all of the streets that normally flood under these conditions to drain properly," said resident Charles Rogers. "Port Monmouth fared well in the storm."[17]

For some, the flood control project came too late. In 2013, Iris Miranda and her family had intended to stay in Port Monmouth for the next eight years. "We really do like it here . . . we have awesome neighbors, awesome. . . . If you need anything, they're there. I love the schools. . . . I like the people around here. . . . Everybody is so nice. . . . And we want to stay." They planned to live in their house until their youngest son, ten years old at the time, graduated from high school. And then? "My next house," said Iris, "will have no water, no ocean, no river, no stream, not a puddle in front of the house." She wanted to live on top of a mountain. "If everything goes well, we'll stick to that plan."[18] Two years later, there was a for-sale sign in their front yard. "The money that my insurance gave me wasn't enough," Iris lamented. "I had to go into my funds. I've got nothing [left]."[19]

It wasn't just post-storm financial insecurity that had impacted the Bayshore; the emotional and psychic trauma lingered as well. For Bob Pulsch, Sandy meant the end of a lifelong hobby. In June 2012, the master boat builder had earned top honors in several regional boat shows for his latest masterpiece, the *Roberta P*, a wooden one-mast catboat named for his beloved wife. The project had taken three years. He had used African sapele for the keel and local white cedar for the planks. Pulsch ("as much historian as craftsman," as the local paper described him) found the design, a 1901 plan by the naval architect Bowdoin B. Crowninshield, in a museum in Peabody, Massachusetts.[20]

The *Star Ledger* published an article on the *Roberta P*'s journey on October 12, just weeks before the storm hit. "I love building boats as much as sailing them," Pulsch was quoted as saying in the piece. The reporter, Charles Zusman, went on, "[Pulsch] often leaves the skippering to his daughter, Susan, a veteran sailor who can 'make the boat dance,' [Pulsch] said."[21] Pulsch had plans to build another boat. He had purchased $1,000 in wood and racked it in his spare shed during his prestorm preparations. The wood came out unscathed. His tools did not. "Maybe someone else wants to build," he said in 2016. "I'm not building anymore big boats. I'm getting too old. . . . I'm [moving on] to model boats."[22]

At their home, the Melfis felt Sandy's effects every time they walked to the front door. "Now that the house is raised," Michael remarked, "we have a lot more stairs to go up. We were very comfortable with the house before the storm." Before Sandy, it was two steps to the front door, two steps to leave. They had planned to retire there. The post-storm changes to their flood insurance forced them to elevate their home. "Now, with all the stairs in the front," Michael continued, "it's a little bit difficult. I think about [it] on a constant daily basis."[23] This was a challenge with particularly resonance for the Bayshore's substantial aging population. "With houses being raised," said Sister Sharon Kelly of the Bayshore Senior Center, "it's harder for [older people] to get in and out." Suddenly, the idea of their forever home felt uncertain.

In Keansburg, one of the most financially vulnerable towns on the Bayshore, the storm's legacy was, perhaps, most noticeable in the absences it created. "Not all the people have returned," said Kelly.[24] More than 1,800 homes in Keansburg were damaged in the storm. Five years later, 500 of them still sat abandoned.[25] "The people hardest hit," Kelly reflected, "were the people who were the poorest, who were renting bungalows near the water."[26] Many of them simply couldn't afford to return. "It's a ghost town," said Mary Edwards, a member of the senior center.[27]

**FIGURE 7.1**   Keansburg Amusement Park gets ready to reopen in spring 2013. January 29, 2013. Photo by Liz Roll/FEMA.

The borough's business district, Kelly noted, was growing. The town had seen new restaurants open, the formation of a local business association, and several focused beautification projects. The boardwalk was restored, and the Gelhaus brothers' amusement park was better than ever. "We're bigger than we were," said Bill. "We have more rides. . . . It's much prettier and up to date. . . . We've positioned ourselves for the future."[28] But those improvements and accolades masked the hundreds of abandoned properties still lining the streets. In some ways, Kelly said, the revitalized shoreline magnified the problem, serving as "a very traumatic reminder of the power of the housed versus those who don't have, and the disparate treatment of that. She added, "I think it will be an open wound on the Jersey shore for years to come."[29]

In October 2017, in the waning days of his second term, Chris Christie came to Keansburg to announce the allocation of $75 million in new funds to the state's Blue Acres program, the initiative through which the government purchased flood-prone properties and reclaimed the land for recreation and conservation. A year earlier, the state had used $284 million of the $300 million allocated funds, securing funding for 846 properties.[30] "This extra infusion of state money," said the governor, "will help the Blue Acres program to convert several hundred more at-risk homes in Keansburg and elsewhere around the state into safe open-space opportunities."[31] For some, the money may have been a welcome relief, a sign that the state was finally paying attention. As the *New York Times* had reported three months earlier, the revival of the Atlantic coast had far outpaced that of the Bayshore. "While the rebuilding has progressed in many communities," wrote *Times* staffer Nick Corasaniti, "there are many others, such as Union Beach, Keyport, and Keansburg on Raritan Bay, where the recovery has been far slower, in part because residents have had to contend with corrupt contractors, insufficient payments from insurers, and miles of red tape."[32]

Bayshore residents would go further. They would tell you that the fixation on the state's tourism industry redirected state and federal funds to the coast, abandoning New Jersey's year-round residents when they were at their most vulnerable. "I can't watch them on television," said Roger Michalak. "There's too much, 'the shore is open, Jersey shore is fixed.' Then how come people aren't in their houses? It was BS. Political bullshit."[33] James Butler understood. Those commercials—Take your family to Wildwood! Come spend money at the shore!—"[they're] kind of tough to swallow when you don't have a house."[34]

The frustration on the Bayshore, Collette Kennedy believed, stemmed from the "lack of ethical standards from the insurance company and the government." People were fed up, she said. "Just last week, a business posted [on Facebook] saying, 'We're Jersey Strong, but not insurance strong. I can't fight them anymore.'" The post included a photo of a for-sale sign.[35] Millie Gonzalez couldn't think of Sandy without remembering Union Beach's Princess Cottage, the famed half-house. Meanwhile, she said, "For New Jersey, the legacy of the storm is the Jersey shore roller coaster in the water. That's what people think of New Jersey. But I think it's bigger than that. . . . I don't want to be [just] the Jersey shore again. I want to be New Jersey again."[36]

**FIGURE 7.2**   The empty lot in Union Beach where the famed Princess Cottage once stood. February 2, 2013. Photo by Sharon Karr/FEMA.

"Jersey Strong." "Stronger than the Storm." The state's post-Sandy slogans left a bad taste along the Bayshore. It was a campaign driven by economics, said Sister Kelly. It benefited the wealthiest beach communities. Towns like Keansburg, Union Beach, and Keyport, she continued, "they're not as good a photo op for some of the politicians."[37] When the history of Sandy is written, said Andrea Bulvid, "it's going to be all about how the Jersey shore was destroyed and how they rebuilt the boardwalk." She continued, "Okay, fine. I'll go to Seaside now. It doesn't smell like puke anymore."[38] Cavallo understood the need to focus on Seaside Heights. He recognized that the state had to get the shore up and running before Memorial Day: "If they weren't ready . . . people might find someplace else to go."[39] But there are consequences—unintended or otherwise—to that sort of tunnel vision. "We're just little old 1.5-square-mile Union Beach," Anthony said, "and we're getting forgotten about."[40]

"They're making it seem like we're okay," said his wife, Jeanne, "when in reality, it's just the big tourist towns that are okay, and we still need help. . . . And people don't realize that when they see the commercials. They're in another state or somewhere else. They think, Oh, everybody is back up and running. Everything is good. We don't need help anymore."[41] For the Cavallos, the slogans brought a particularly cruel irony. The damage to their home had been so catastrophic, in part, because it was built of cinderblock, a material far less forgiving and flexible than a wood-frame house. "My house," said Anthony, "broke because it was"—a pause—"stronger than the storm."[42]

Still, amidst the frustration, financial insecurity, abandoned properties, and changing Bayshore skyline, what might be the most enduring legacies of the storm were the relationships forged in its wake. "I didn't really know that many people in my neighborhood," recalled Adam Bixby of life before October 2012. He and his wife were younger than everyone else on their block. They didn't have any reason to connect, he said. "But after the storm, I know pretty much everybody . . . I feel more a part of the community now." Linda Gonzalez took that further. The storm buoyed her faith in the broader society: "The whole country came to our rescue, and that gives me hope."[43]

Sandy's story, said Project PAUL's Sal Cortale, is two-fold. It is, without question, a story of the devastation, "unbelievable damage and destruction . . . and tremendous sadness and aggravation." At the same time, "you had this outpouring of the community coming together. . ., everybody coming together and pulling together to help a community, New Jersey, pull itself back together."[44] Sister Kelly concluded, "[We learned] that we are stronger together."[45]

On November 6, 2018, Collette Kennedy became the first woman ever to be elected mayor of Keyport. Her bid began in the weeks and months after the storm, as the scope of the damage and the resilience of the community were laid bare. She ran her campaign on the promise to bring transparency to municipal government and to usher in policies to ensure that the borough ran smoothly and effectively. Her motto during her first term? "The more we planned and prepared, the less people would panic."[46] That language held particular resonance for those who had lived through Sandy. The storm had unmasked the true toll of catastrophic weather, and it had demonstrated the capacity for resilience and compassion that can emerge in its wake.

# LIST OF INTERVIEWS

All interviews from the Staring Out to Sea Oral History Project are housed digitally at the Louie B. Nunn Center for Oral History at the University of Kentucky. The interviews appear here arranged in alphabetical order by narrator's last name.

Bednarczyk, Lara. Interview by Trudi-Ann Lawrence. August 10, 2013.
Bixby, Adam. Interview by Brittany Le Strange. May 24, 2013.
Bixby, Adam. Interview by Ruqayyah Abdullah. May 15, 2015.
Bulvid, Andrea. Interview by Trudi-Ann Lawrence. June 5, 2013.
Butler, James. Interview by Trudi-Ann Lawrence. July 11, 2013.
Cavallo, Anthony. Interview by Trudi-Ann Lawrence. August 20, 2013.
Cortale, Sal. Interview by Brittany Le Strange. June 19, 2013.
Cortale, Sal. Interview by Abigail Perkiss. May 27, 2015.
Crook, Mary. Interview by Trudi-Ann Lawrence. September 3, 2013.
Crook, Mary. Interview by Ruqayyah Abdullah. March 19, 2015.
DeFilippis, Jeremy. Interview by Mary Piasecki. January 1, 2014.
DeFilippis, Jeremy. Interview by Abigail Perkiss. May 12, 2015.
Disbrow, Diana. Interview by Trudi-Ann Lawrence. August 10, 2013.
Dorr, Angelita. Interview by Britany Le Strange. March 22, 2013.
Dunlea, Mike. Interview by Brittany Le Strange. August 1, 2013.
Dunlea, Mike. Interview by Christina Leedy. August 26, 2015.
Edwards, Mary. Interview by Trudi-Ann Lawrence. September 9, 2013.

Edwards, Mary. Interview by Ruqayyah Abdullah. March 19, 2015.

Evans, George. Interview by Trudi-Ann Lawrence. July 13, 2014.

Fiorenzo, Christina. Interview by Trudi-Ann Lawrence. August 10, 2013.

Gajewski, Dorothy and Robert. Interview by Trudi-Ann Lawrence. August 28, 2013.

Gelhaus, William. Interview by Trudi-Ann Lawrence. September 4, 2013.

Gonzalez, Linda, and Melissa Manzi. Interview by Trudi-Ann Lawrence. March 20, 2013.

Gonzalez, Millie. Interview by Trudi-Ann Lawrence. June 12, 2013.

Hill, Alicia. Interview by Brittany Le Strange. March 5, 2013.

Hill, Alicia. Interview by Abigail Perkiss. May 28, 2015.

Kelly, Sharon. Interview by Trudi-Ann Lawrence. September 4, 2013.

Kelly, Sharon. Interview by Ruqayyah Abdullah. May 28, 2015.

Kennedy, Collette. Interview by Trudi-Ann Lawrence. December 16, 2013.

Kennedy, Collette. Interview by Abigail Perkiss. May 28, 2015.

Kiely, Karen. Interview by Trudi-Ann Lawrence. December 6, 2013.

Kiely, Karen. Interview by Abigail Perkiss. June 8, 2015.

Lawrence, Trudi-Ann. Interview by Arij Syed. March 7, 2013.

Lawrence, Trudi-Ann. Interview by Abigail Perkiss. June 17, 2015.

Le Strange, Brittany. Interview by Abdelfatth Rasheed. March 4, 2013.

Le Strange, Brittany. Interview by Abigail Perkiss. June 11, 2015.

Mangino, Joe. Interview by Brittany Le Strange. July 18, 2013.

Mangino, Joe. Interview by Christina Leedy. July 13, 2015.

Mara, Cheryl. Interview by Trudi-Ann Lawrence. August 26, 2013.

Mara, Cheryl. Interview by Ruqayyah Abdullah. May 19, 2015.

Melfi, Joann and Michael. Interview by Mary Piasecki. September 24, 2013.

Michalak, Mary Jane, and Roger Michalak. Interview by Trudi-Ann Lawrence. October 23, 2013.

Miranda, Iris. Interview by Trudi-Ann Lawrence. May 15, 2013.

Miranda, Iris. Interview by Ruqayyah Abdullah. May 15, 2015.

O'Halleran, Kathleen. Interview by Brittany Le Strange. June 19, 2013.

Perroth, Glen. Interview by Arij Syed. March 25, 2013.

Piasecki, Mary. Interview by Alicia Hill. March 7, 2013.

Piasecki, Mary. Interview by Abigail Perkiss. May 19, 2015.

Piasecki, Maureen, and John Piasecki. Interview by Alicia Hill. March 25, 2013.

Pulsch, Robert. Interview by Brittany Le Strange. May 16, 2013.

Pulsch, Robert. Interview by Ruqayyah Abdullah. March 19, 2015.

Rasheed, Abdelfatth. Interview by Trudi-Ann Lawrence. March 5, 2013.

Rasheed, Abdelfatth. Interview by Abigail Perkiss. May 20, 2015.

Rivera, Nelson. Interview by Ruqayyah Abdullah. December 12, 2013.

Rivera, Nelson. Interview by Ruqayyah Abdullah. May 26, 2015.

Sefchek, Barbara. Interview by Trudi-Ann Lawrence. May 21, 2013.

Sefchek, Barbara. Interview by Ruqayyah Abdullah. May 5, 2015.

Smith, Paul. Interview by Trudi-Ann Lawrence. September 4, 2013.

Smith, Paul. Interview by Abigail Perkiss. June 4, 2015.

Syed, Arij. Interview by Mary Piasecki. February 28, 2013.

Syed, Arij. Interview by Abigail Perkiss. May 18, 2015.

Willem, Nick. Interview by Mary Piasecki. March 24, 2013.

Williams, Henrietta. Interview by Trudi-Ann Lawrence. September 3, 2013.

Williams, Henrietta. Interview by Ruqayyah Abdullah. March 19, 2015.

# Appendix B

## HURRICANE SANDY ON NEW JERSEY'S FORGOTTEN SHORE: AN ORIGINS STORY

This book was born out of an unexpected phone call from my graduate school colleague and good friend, Kate Scott, then the assistant historian at the US Senate Historical Office and the secretary of Oral History in the Mid-Atlantic Region (OHMAR), the regional arm of the national Oral History Association, in early December 2012.[1]

"Abby," she said when I picked up my cell from my office at Kean University. "I'm wondering if you know anyone up in New Jersey who might be conducting oral histories on Hurricane Sandy. OHMAR would be interested in providing support for such a project."

I didn't, but I told her that I welcomed the chance to do it myself. Although I had substantial experience and training in interviewing and had used oral history methods in my own research and teaching, I had never directed a large-scale project. The prospect of doing so on such a timely and important topic and with the support and guidance of OHMAR sounded like the perfect entry point.

When I hung up, I walked down to my department chair's office. "What do you think of a Hurricane Sandy oral history project?" I asked him. He was, as I expected, supportive—and strategic. He knew, as I did, the challenges of such an undertaking. Resources were limited, and the timeline was tight. With my heavy teaching load—four classes each semester—and substantial service responsibilities, not to mention a four-hour round-trip commute up and down the New Jersey Turnpike between my home in Philadelphia and Kean, we both questioned how I would be able to conduct such time-sensitive interviews efficiently and effectively.

We were also both aware of the inherent value of this work and the potential opportunities it might pose for our students. We decided that I should use the classroom as a sandbox for the project. That spring, I would collaborate with a group of students to craft the parameters of the work, build a list of narrators, and begin the interview process. The class would culminate with a student-led presentation at the annual OHMAR conference the following April. Five minutes later, I walked out of his office with a new research agenda, a new pedagogical challenge, and only six weeks before the start of the spring semester.

Over the next month, I reached out to several seasoned oral historians—Linda Shopes, Don Ritchie, Stephen Sloan, and D'Ann Penner—who offered guidance on how to develop such a project. We spoke about the time-sensitive nature of the research, the need for clarity in the goals and objectives of the work, and the importance of creating a longitudinal framework in order to chart the relief and recovery efforts of the storm beyond the immediate crisis. The willingness of these scholars to provide counsel was instrumental in my own development as an oral historian, and it was critical to the success of the student researchers.

When the course met for the first time, on January 24, 2013, I encountered a group of students who were eager to begin developing an oral history project about an issue still rapidly unfolding, both around them and within their own lives. Some of them had experienced only minor damage to their homes; for others, however, the storm had wreaked havoc on their families and communities, and they were still in the early stages of rebuilding. This was true not only for the students in the class but also for Kean University more broadly. Kean is home to a diverse student body and a significant commuter population. The majority are the first in their families to go to college. Those enrolled at Kean balance heavy course loads with substantial out-of-class work and family responsibilities. For many, the storm threw their precarious stability into chaos. Students living in dorms were forced to leave campus for ten days, after the infrastructure of the university's electrical system was compromised. At home, many experienced lengthy power outages, substantial property damage, and the inability to travel to campus (once operations did resume) because of statewide gas shortages. This was the reality that many of our students had been living since the storm and the reality that we would have to make sense of in the months to come.

At our first meeting, we sat in a circle and recounted our own experiences with Sandy. Four of the students in the class spoke of downed power lines and uprooted trees, of brief disruptions in service, of a storm that passed through and left few lingering effects. For two students, however, Sandy had brought terror to their homes and families. Living in New Jersey's Bayshore community, directly across the Sandy Hook Bay from New York's Staten Island, Brittany Le Strange and Mary Piasecki had seen their streets flood, their houses fill with water, and many of their possessions destroyed. Le Strange cried as she recounted sitting on the stairs in her home and watching the water rise through the first floor of the house. It was at that moment that I began to understand the transformative potential of this project. This work would reach far beyond a pedagogical exercise for these students. It would be an opportunity for them to give voice to their own experiences and the experiences of their friends and neighbors as they recalibrated their lives.

During the first several weeks of the semester, we read about the history of oral history and disaster. Through the work of Studs Terkel, Mary Marshall Clark, and Stephen Sloan, the students began to get a sense of the challenges that come with conducting interviews in the midst of catastrophe. We talked at length about what narrators could teach us about disaster response, the recovery process, and the relationships between government and communities. We discussed how we would reach people who had been displaced by the storm and how we could responsibly bring them back into their experiences of Sandy without subjecting them to further trauma.

By late February, after lengthy conversations about the stories we hoped to capture and the tone we sought to evoke with the project, we had arrived at the project title—Staring Out to Sea (owing to one student's fondness for alliteration)—and we determined that we wanted to focus the project around questions of power, access, and representation in the wake of the storm. How do we respond to such devastation? What is the role of government in providing relief? What is the role of civil society? Of individuals? How do issues of race and socioeconomic status impact recovery efforts? Whose voices matter? Who feels heard?

We also wanted to put the story of Sandy in conversation with other disaster relief efforts in the United States. Like Katrina before it, Sandy required local, state, and federal resources for both immediate and long-term rehabilitation. How could our findings contribute to a growing body of literature on twenty-first-century disaster testimonies, during a time of rapidly evolving governmental systems and procedures, a new global age of terror, and the increasing ferocity of storms? What could we learn from the response to Sandy? How could we use Sandy as a model for disaster relief in the future? It was a lofty undertaking for six New Jersey undergraduates.

And so we set to work. We developed themes and questions. We focused our study on the Bayshore and worked on narrator recruitment, relying heavily on the local knowledge of Le Strange and Piasecki to build a list of interviewees. As a group, the students made presentations at community meetings and used the process of snowball sampling to expand the network and foster relationships with subjects. On March 21, 2013, Piasecki stood in front of two hundred Port Monmouth residents at a contentious community meeting, during which people expressed deep frustrations over the lack of response from local officials and demanded greater planning and infrastructure before the next storm.[2] Piasecki was, for many, a welcome break in the yelling, and attendees were appreciative and supportive when she told them about the project and invited them to participate. During her presentation, she shed the language of victimization that had become a common refrain in the class, and instead spoke of those who had lived through the storm as survivors. She counted herself among them.[3] Later that evening, Piasecki reflected on the responsibility she felt in making the presentation: "It is quite hard to capture the emotion I was feeling as these residents approached me and knowing that I had the power to make their voices heard. I intend to include all of these residents, and whoever else wishes to be involved in our project. While we have merely started down this road, my classmates and I are committed to our project and will work to make our interviewees heard."[4]

At the end of the meeting, the students collected names and information from several homeowners and made a plan to contact them in the coming days. Several of the people they met that evening were later interviewed for the project.

We also brought in experts on the Institutional Review Board process, interviewing, and fieldwork, and, for one particularly useful session, oral history and trauma. Kean Associate Professor of Psychology Dr. Jennifer Lerner and doctoral student Lindsay Liotta discussed the risks of trauma in postdisaster situations, the distinctions between counseling and oral history, and the need to recognize the impact of trauma on both interviewee and interviewer.[5] At the same time, the students practiced their interview skills, pairing off and recording interviews with each other, which we then analyzed collectively in class.

Throughout the entire process, students were assigned the task of blogging about the experience of developing the project.[6] The blog was meant to offer them a space for reflection about both the process of learning oral history and their work on the project itself. The students were required to post at least three times during the semester to chronicle and capture their individual and collective experiences and, because the blog was open to public readership, to develop a consciousness surrounding digital literacy about the public function of the project. The blog was conceived ultimately to become a part of the permanent Staring Out to Sea website, which would include a special section on pedagogy and process. Although we routinely discussed the work we were undertaking in class, the blog also became a space for me to gain insights into the way they were experiencing the class, the work they were doing, and their relationship with the storm.

As Arij Syed later wrote of the process:

> A certain level of responsibility comes along with the task of document-ing history. To ensure the validity of this documentation, it is impor-tant to follow standards that maintain credibility. Working with actual real people adds another level of responsibility. When you relive events, especially traumatic events, you also relive how you felt at that time. This brings forth the question, how do you ethically deal with emo-tional people? Our task as oral historians is to most accurately cap-ture an event in history through transcribing interviews with people who lived through the event. Strong emotional reactions however can change how someone may retell that event.... Our project especially has to focus on this as Hurricane Sandy victims have [been] through severe trauma. It has been a truly enlightening experience learning how to bal-ance creating an accurate primary historical source, while at the same time doing justice to the stories of Sandy's disaster victims.[7]

Syed's comments reflect the students' experience in going through this intensive training; in learning the process and practice of oral history, they began to appre-ciate both the challenge and responsibility of doing oral history work.

Finally, they were ready to go into the field. Each student was assigned the task of conducting and transcribing one interview with a resident of the Bayshore. For most of them, these interviews offered the first opportunity to travel to the area since the storm. This exposure proved critical in shaping their experience, as they were able to connect the stories with the destruction they were seeing in the neighborhoods. These early interviews also became important beta tests; several of the students came back with ideas for new questions and new lines of inquiry for future interviews.[8] The six interviews they conducted became the foundation for the project, which ultimately expanded to nearly fifty narrators and close to seventy interviews.

The final phase of the course took students through the transcription process. As a group, they listened to interview clips from various oral history collections and tried to transcribe the conversations on site. Then, they compared their tran-script with the polished transcriptions of those clips, paying particular attention to the impact that editorial interpretation can have on the final product. Using the Baylor University style guide for oral history transcription, students then set out to transcribe their peer and field interviews.

As the students were conducting and transcribing interviews, I started to look ahead to the next phase of the project. Through the spring and summer of 2013,

I worked with Kean's Office of Research and Sponsored Programs to apply for more than $100,000 in internal and external grants. Our aim was to expand the semester-long project into a longitudinal study and to develop an online digital repository for the interviews that we had already conducted.

At the end of the semester, the students and I traveled to College Park, Maryland to present at the 2013 OHMAR Conference. We spent the first day attending other panels, and in listening to the presentations of more established scholars, the students at first expressed anxiety about their own panel the following morning. They worried that they would come across as amateurs, that they would get flustered, that they wouldn't measure up. As they moved through the day, however, and were able to connect with other attendees, and as those other attendees treated them as members of the OHMAR community, the students began to see themselves as similarly situated professionals.

That evening, the group continued preparations for their own presentation. Although it quickly became apparent that they had not appreciated the professional nature of the conference and the differences between speaking to their classmates and speaking before a professional community, the long night proved to be an opportunity for growth for the students. After a tense conversation about the nature of the next day's panel and an honest critique of the state of their remarks, they retreated to their hotel rooms, rewriting and revising for hours. The following morning, we gathered in the hotel breakfast room for one last run-through of their remarks. As they rehearsed over bagels and Belgian waffles, their commitment to improvement became clear. Through a combination of peer pressure and tough love from me, they had developed a measured, nuanced, and sophisticated presentation that would lead their audience through the process of developing the project.

When they took the stage of the large auditorium on Friday morning for the premiere panel of that slot, they spoke eloquently about their experience, first describing the origins of the project, then taking the attendees through the early phases of implementation. They divided the various parts of the presentation among them. Piasecki and Alicia Hill discussed the oral history boot camp that they had experienced early in the semester and the process through which we had crafted the Staring Out to Sea project. Abdelfatth Rasheed addressed the trauma training they had undertaken and the extent to which it prepared them for conducting their own interviews. Rasheed, the only second-semester senior in the group, had at times been less connected to the project, as he focused on what was to come after graduation. But he found the discussions of trauma to be particularly compelling, and he spoke eloquently about the need to pay attention to the rhetorical and visual cues that the narrator might offer in displaying early signs of retraumatization during the interview. Le Strange and Trudi-Ann Lawrence spoke of their roles as both insiders and outsiders in the project, outlining the different experiences among the students who lived through the storm on the Bayshore and those who bore witness to the destruction through their interviews.

Finally, Arij Syed offered a preliminary analysis of the interview findings: the sense of abandonment by the federal government that many who had been impacted by Sandy felt, the overwhelming strength and interconnectedness of their communities, the generosity of the volunteers, the sensationalized media coverage, the challenges of participating in the political process (particularly the 2012 presidential election, which took place just days after the storm), and the near-universal support for New Jersey governor Chris Christie. In synthesizing the students' early interviews, Syed spoke deliberately, careful to reflect the limited time that they had had for analysis and interpretation and the limited scope of the project to that point.

Audience members responded enthusiastically, asking challenging questions and offering high praise for the student presenters. The presentation was notable for many reasons, commenters remarked, but particularly impressive was the amount of work the students had accomplished in such a short amount of time. Attendees noted that in just a few months, the undergraduates had turned into experienced project developers, and they had been able to convey that process to a group of practiced professionals and scholars.

For Le Strange, the presentation provided the affirmation of the intensive work that had been done over the previous three months. As she reflected: "Having the opportunity to present at the OHMAR conference is an experience that I will never forget. I was so excited to go to College Park and the closer it got the more scared I became. It was amazing to sit there and present and see these historians excited about our project and the work we had accomplished. I do not know how any of us could have made it better."[9]

The conference brought with it a sense of profound satisfaction, Le Strange implied, in large part because the stakes had been so high. Unlike a traditional classroom experience, where the semester culminates in a final paper or exam, here, the students were required to present publicly a body of work that had become intensely personal for them. In sharing the project and receiving such a warm response, Le Strange received more than a grade on her transcript; she found renewed value in the work she and her fellow students were doing.

The students' work in developing Staring Out to Sea opened new professional doors to them. In the months that followed our semester together, three of the original six students (Lawrence, Le Strange, and Piasecki) took on internships at the Tuckerton Seaport and Baymen's Museum in southern New Jersey. At Tuckerton, they were responsible for creating a public exhibit about Sandy recovery, which included a StoryCorps-like interview booth for visitors to share their own experiences with the storm.[10] At the same time, the three conducted interviews in and around Tuckerton, expanding the original geographic scope of Staring Out to Sea to the southern New Jersey coastline. In October, we traveled together to Oklahoma City to present with Kate Scott at the 2013 Oral History Association annual meeting. Our session focused on the institutional partnerships that both fostered and were fostered by the project.

That same month, the students saw their work featured in the American Historical Association's *Perspectives on History* magazine. An article by Jennifer Reut described the development of Staring Out to Sea and highlighted the intensive work that the students had done. "In April," Reut wrote, "the class presented at the OHMAR conference in College Park, Maryland, and students wrote candidly [on the class blog] about the difficulty in balancing their own emotional response to the trauma with their purpose of communicating professionally about their project. Others were excited to be presenting their original research at an academic conference among experts, a first for many, if not all, the undergraduates."[11] Her piece reflected the growth that the students experienced through the project. It also confirmed for them the value of the work they were doing outside of the walls of their classroom. In the weeks that followed, Kean University promoted the project, heralding them as scholarly and community ambassadors for the school.

Like any public history project, Staring Out to Sea encountered challenges. First, the speed at which the project first emerged meant that the students received basic training in all aspects of oral history but specialized and advanced training in none. This was particularly clear in the transcription phase of the project, when a combination of lack of time (the students were, by that time in the semester, beyond the OHMAR presentation and were increasingly focusing on finals preparation in their other classes) and lack of rigorous training led to relatively sloppy transcriptions. I spent an untold number of hours reviewing and revising the completed documents. Students also grappled with issues of subject recruitment, as Bayshore residents, tending to their immediate material and emotional recovery, were reluctant or unable to participate in programs to document and chronicle the aftermath of the storm. And even as students brought their project to a wider audience with their curatorial work at Tuckerton, the original oral history component of the project shrank in scope because of limited funding. Though we began with the intention of collecting one hundred hours of tape, by the time Lawrence, Le Strange, and Piasecki completed their internships, the project consisted of only fifteen to twenty hours.

At the same time, though the original six students were deeply committed to the project, over the next two semesters, as they moved forward toward graduation and life beyond Kean, their focus shifted and their time and ability to stay involved waned. I also learned that none of the $100,000 in grant funding had come to fruition. Though I did not receive concrete feedback from all funders, those that did offer comment noted the abstract nature of the digital library and the lack of a concrete plan for implementation of the longitudinal nature of the project as the key problems in the proposal.

But an ever-expanding network manifested in renewed energy and new opportunities for developing the next phase of the project. In the summer of 2014, Dan Royles, then a visiting professor of history at Richard Stockton University in New Jersey (and another good friend from graduate school), approached me about using the project as a focal point for his undergraduate digital humanities course. That fall, as I worked feverishly to transcribe the remaining interviews and Royles reviewed and processed the transcriptions, he trained his students in the technology of the Oral History Metadata Synchronizer (OHMS) and WordPress and worked with them to index the transcribed interviews and build out a prototype of the digital library. By semester's end, the class had developed not only a rough site but also design plans for the final version. One of Royles's students, Chelsea Mendoza, stayed on the following spring, completing indexes for all of the interviews while receiving independent study credit. That same spring, several students from Kean's computer programming department took on the Staring Out to Sea web presence as a class project, developing the site and integrating OHMS functionality. Meanwhile, Royles and I successfully applied for additional grants—from the New Jersey Council for the Humanities and the New Jersey Historical Commission—to complete the website and conduct and transcribe follow-up interviews with all willing narrators.

In many critical ways, this project was highly particularized; it was born out of a unique combination of circumstances, relationships, and personnel, and it was supported by a variety of institutions at every step of the development process. The early and continued commitment from Kean University, OHMAR, and the Oral History Association—and later Richard Stockton University, the New Jersey Council for the Humanities, and the New Jersey Historical Commission—led to the creation of an important community oral history project and, no less significant, the development of a new and emerging group of oral and public historians, trained and practiced in oral history and digital humanities methods. This distinctive set of resources came together to create the possibility for meaningful oral history work where the whole was much greater than the sum of its individual parts.

At the same time, this project reveals the potential that arises when institutions come together to pool their financial, experiential, and temporal resources toward a collective end. Oral and public history work is built on collaboration, creativity, and adaptability in the face of limited time and personnel and increasingly diminishing financial support. Staring Out to Sea offers a model for the ways in which individual agencies and organizations can come together to support the development of new and innovative projects that serve the interests of both public historians and the communities with which they work. Taken to scale, this project offers the framework for ongoing, sustainability oral history work at all levels of the profession.

# Appendix C

# STUDENT REFLECTIONS

The Staring Out to Sea Oral History Project was developed in an advanced undergraduate oral history methods seminar at Kean University in the spring of 2013. Six students enrolled in the class, and each was instrumental in the development and growth of the project. Later, two additional Kean students joined us as interviewers. The Staring Out to Sea team includes Ruqayyah Abdullah, Alicia Hill, Trudi-Ann Lawrence, Christina Leedy, Brittany Le Strange, Mary Piasecki, Abdelfatth Rasheed, and Arij Syed.

In fall 2014, students from Dan Royles's digital humanities class at Stockton University joined the project, indexing each of the recordings to make them accessible for a wider audience. These students include Max Alpert, Rachel Archer, Savannah Demko, Russell Ernst, Jennifer Hanley, Chelsey Mendoza, Jacqueline Muhlbaier, Richard Pisani, Kirolos Sadallah, and Margaux Terhune.

Two of the student interviewers, Trudi-Ann Lawrence and Arij Syed, wrote essays in the summer of 2018 about their Staring Out to Sea experience. In them, they reflected on the project and the impact that it had on their lives and professional plans. For more on the effect of this project, and of oral history work more broadly, on undergraduate interviewers, see Abigail Perkiss, "Staring Out to Sea and the Transformative Power of Oral History for Undergraduate Interviewers," *Oral History Review* 43, no. 2 (September 2016): 392–407.

For more voices from the student interviewers, visit the digital archive of the project at the Louie B. Nunn Center for Oral History at the University of Kentucky.

# Trudi-Ann Lawrence: August 27, 2018

At the time of the storm, I was still very young and, in a sense, naive. I lived in my own little world. I wasn't too concerned about anyone or anything that didn't directly affect me. It wasn't intentional—I just hadn't had any need to look beyond that. When I started working on the Staring Out to Sea project and going into the towns that faced devastation, that's when things started to take on a different meaning for me. I began to imagine how it would feel if those were my homes and my towns. I have an evocative imagination so when individuals and families would share their stories with me, I would visualize every aspect. This really put everything in perspective for me. I began to empathize, and it allowed me to feel what they were feeling: the hurts, the emotions, and the turmoil. I became more understanding of their plight.

My sense of being considerate of people who have been affected by a natural disaster was heightened. Often, I found that people were leery of agreeing to do the interview because they felt as though news outlets and media sources had capitalized on their story and failed to take into consideration their struggles. People felt exploited and shared with me that they didn't want to talk to people unless they were truly willing to listen. This was a vulnerable time for people, as they lost their homes and a great deal of privacy. I was shocked when I heard that days following the storms, towns were on lockdown because houses were left wide open and this made them prone to looting.

Working in the field, interviewing people, was my favorite part of the whole experience. I loved talking to and meeting so many of those impacted by the storm. I loved offering them an outlet where they were able to share their story, especially because so many people felt forgotten. Some felt as though they were going through this experience alone and they had no support. I felt that I was able to give these people a voice when I traveled to College Park, Maryland, to present at the OHMAR conference—it was our way of sharing and honoring what they experienced. At one point, I was so moved by their stories that it led me to tears during our presentation.

In addition to interviewing people, I also had the opportunity to work as an intern at the Tuckerton Seaport and Baymen's Museum. While there, one of my classmates and I created an exhibit dedicated to the people who were affected by Superstorm Sandy. This exhibit created another outlet where people could share their stories, and it gave us a sense of pride in being able to represent the people who felt like they weren't adequately represented. During this time, I got to interview more families and tour the area.

One of the most memorable interviews I did there was with the mayor of Tuckerton. Interviewing him only made my heart grow bigger. I couldn't believe I was speaking with someone of so much power and presence. One thing I remember most about that experience was the thought that even though he was such an important person, he was also human just like everyone else. I remember when we went around the town and he showed me his house. I was expecting a mansion far away on a hill, but in actuality, he lived on a common street between two other residences. He, too, had been displaced and had to relocate. He, too, was facing the issues others had faced with insurance companies. Seeing this truly made a difference for me. It reminded me that even those who carry such power and presence are not excluded from life's challenges.

This project was life changing for me. It showed me another way of doing history. Talking to people and interviewing them taught me so much more than I could have ever learned from any news outlet. I gained a stronger sense of empathy toward others because I understood their pain, struggles, and successes. Whenever I see a natural disaster broadcast on television, as with Hurricane Harvey in 2017, my thoughts immediately go to those people and what they are experiencing. While working in the field, I would walk into an interview with a stranger and leave feeling as though they were family. The feeling I had as these people shared their stories, inviting me into their homes when they were most vulnerable, is indelibly printed on my mind.

I have worked on various leadership projects and have served on various executive boards, but this project was the most exciting and exhilarating work I have been a part of. During Staring Out to Sea, I was often asked, "Do you think this is something you would want to do in the future?" I always battled with that question because I was in school for elementary special education. I had no clue how to utilize this project and bridge oral history with my passion for teaching history to young students. Now that I've gained a better idea of what oral historians do, I am still very intrigued. Though I still have not figured out what role oral history will play in my professional life, I am confident that oral history is something I want to pursue after my chapter of teaching ends.

If I could share one message regarding this project it would be, "When a natural disaster strikes, think about the people and what they are going through." I think that this sentiment is often forgotten. But I know that I will always think of the people first and put their feelings above anything else. I'm grateful to have been able to work on such a life-changing project. I do not think that I would have developed such a heart of compassion without this work. I am a better person today thanks to Staring Out to Sea.

# Arij Syed: July 31, 2018

History has multiple perspectives: the perspective of the person documenting it; the perspective of the person writing about it; the perspective of the person studying it; and the last and most elusive perspective, that of the person living it. Through my involvement in the Staring Out to Sea Oral History Project I had the privilege of experiencing the perspective of someone who lived through what is arguably the worst natural disaster in the history of the state of New Jersey.

As a history student you read a lot. A lot. You read about kings and empires, wars and revolutions, prophets and politicians. But history goes beyond books, too. Through Staring Out to Sea, I wasn't just reading anymore. I was doing. I was actually taking part in documenting history. Real history about real people. No agenda. No bias. No profit. This was for the culture. For "History." For the ability to be part of something and record it for the future.

I remember the extensive training the team did preparing for the actual interviews. We were getting ready to relive a person's trauma with them, and we had to be able to respond to them in a way that was both clinical and empathetic, while at the same time making sure we got a good interview. This was no easy task. Imagine watching the first floor of your house steadily fill with water. Then going for over a week without electricity when the water finally recedes. Now imagine talking about the whole ordeal in detail to a complete stranger you just met, only a short period of time after it happened. It can get emotional.

I remember my interview with Glenn Perroth vividly. His family was hit quite hard by the storm. They took on four and a half feet of water. They had fish swimming in their living room. They had to rebuild the entire first floor. However, during the interview, Mr. Perroth was calm and composed. His answers were direct and to the point. He didn't embellish. A central theme emerged from our conversation: the storm happened and he dealt with it. His family was there when we talked and contributed to the interview as well, helping to fill in details. As expected, they were more emotional in their retelling of this traumatic experience. Still, Mr. Perroth remained stoic. And maybe he had to be. Mr. Perroth did have a lot to say about the politics around the storm. He spoke at length on the reelection campaigns of Chris Christie and Barack Obama, and the governmental aid—or lack thereof—that was available for the victims of the storm. It became clear to me that the storm and the government's response had an effect on both upcoming elections. And it should have. People make the decisions that they do because of the circumstances that they are in, and only they can truly understand those circumstances, because no one else has lived them. This is especially important now, after our most recent presidential election. It happened for a reason. This project taught me that people may have a different world view than you, but that world view was formed by the specific circumstances that happened in their lives. The only way to understand that world view is to walk in their shoes and experience what they have experienced. Oral history offers us an opportunity to experience that unique perspective.

As the person asking questions, you have to remember the dynamic with the narrator. You are asking questions about an event, but it is not just an event to the interviewee. It is their life. They lived this, and you have to respect that. It is not history for them. They are allowing you take a chapter from their story and preserve it for the ages, and trusting you to do it right. That is a privilege. As I write this, it's about to be six years since the storm. Today I am an attorney and every day I am reminded of this privilege whenever I talk to a client or litigant in court.

# Notes

## PREFACE

1. Michalis Diakakis et al., "Hurricane Sandy Mortality in the Caribbean and Continental North America," *Disaster Prevention and Management* 24, no. 1 (2015): 137.

2. "Situation Report" (Washington, DC: US Department of Energy, November 7, 2012), https://www.energy.gov/articles/responding-hurricane-sandy-doe-situation-reports; David Sheppard and Scott DiSavino, "Superstorm Sandy Cuts Power to 8.1 Million Homes," Reuters, October 30, 2012, https://www.reuters.com/article/us-storm-sandy-powercuts/superstorm-sandy-cuts-power-to-8-1-million-homes-idUS BRE89T10G20121030.

3. Fair Share Housing Center, Latino Action Network, and NAACP New Jersey State Conference, "The State of Sandy Recovery: Second Annual Report," February 2015, 1, http://fairsharehousing.org/images/uploads/State_of_Sandy_English_2015.pdf.

4. Joseph Bilinski et al., "Damage Assessment Report on the Effects of Hurricane Sandy on the State of New Jersey's Natural Resources" (Trenton: Office of Science, New Jersey Department of Environmental Protection, May 2015), 7, https://www.nj.gov/dep/dsr/hurricane-sandy-assessment.pdf. Copy in author's possession.

5. For more on climate change and sea level rise in relation to hurricane frequency, see chapter 6.

6. "Underwater: Rising Seas, Chronic Floods, and the Implications for US Coastal Real Estate" (Cambridge, MA: Union of Concerned Scientists, 2018), https://www.ucsusa.org/sites/default/files/attach/2018/06/underwater-analysis-full-report.pdf. Copy in author's possession.

7. "Underwater."

8. James K. Mitchell, "A Century of Natural Disasters in a State of Changing Vulnerability," in *New Jersey's Environments: Past, Present, and Future*, ed. Neil Maher (New Brunswick, NJ: Rutgers University Press, 2006), 165.

9. For more on oral history as a process of recovery, see Mary Marshall Clark, "Case Study: Field Notes on Catastrophe; Reflections on the September 11, 2001, Oral History Memory and Narrative Project," *The Oxford Handbook of Oral History*, ed. Donald A. Ritchie (New York: Oxford University Press, 2018). See also Kristi Girdharry, "Organizational Sponsorship: An Ethical Framework for Community Oral History Projects," *Oral History Review* 48, no. 2 (2021): 246–57.

10. For more on this oral history project, see appendix B.

11. Some scholarship suggests possibilities for using oral history as a way to connect to and capture the voices of the natural world. See Debbie Lee and Kathryn Newfont, eds., *New Voices at the Intersection of Oral and Environmental History* (New York: Oxford University Press, 2017).

## 1. FRANKENSTORM

1. Collette Kennedy, in discussion with the author, April 17, 2017. In April 2017, following her second oral history interview with the Staring Out to Sea team, Kennedy invited me to visit her home. After recounting again her own experience during and after Sandy, she took me on a tour of the Bayshore, nearly five years after the storm struck.

2. Collette Kennedy, interview by Trudi-Ann Lawrence, December 16, 2013, Staring Out to Sea: Hurricane Sandy Oral History Project, Louie B. Nunn Center for Oral History, University of Kentucky Libraries, Lexington, https://kentuckyoralhistory.org/ark:/16417/xt7m0c4sn30n.

3. Kathryn Miles, *Superstorm: Nine Days inside Hurricane Sandy* (New York: Dutton, 2014), 47. Miles's book chronicles the week preceding the storm and culminates in Sandy's collision with the Eastern Seaboard. Her detailed reporting was invaluable to the development of this chapter.

4. Kennedy interview, December 16, 2013.

5. New Jersey has 127 miles of shoreline along the Atlantic Ocean and an additional 83 miles on the Raritan and Delaware Bays. New Jersey Department of Environmental Protection, Division of Coastal Engineering, http://www.nj.gov/dep/shoreprotection/, accessed March 7, 2016.

6. Richard Lathrop and John Hasse, "Tracking New Jersey's Changing Landscape," in *New Jersey's Environments: Past, Present, and Future*, ed. Neil Maher (New Brunswick, NJ: Rutgers University Press, 2006), 122; Adam Sobel, *Storm Surge: Hurricane Sandy, Our Changing Climate, and Extreme Weather of the Past and Future* (New York: Harper Wave, 2014), xviii.

7. Sobel, *Storm Surge*, xix.

8. Eric Blake et al., "Tropical Cyclone Report: Hurricane Sandy" (Miami: National Hurricane Center, February 12, 2013), http://www.nhc.noaa.gov/data/tcr/AL182012_Sandy.pdf, accessed May 11, 2016; Miles, *Superstorm*, 106.

9. Sarah Rainsford, "Hurricane Sandy: Cuba Struggles to Help Those Hit," *BBC News*, November 12, 2012, http://www.bbc.com/news/world-latin-america-20294006.

10. Miles, *Superstorm*, 1.

11. Mike Esterl et al., "Monster Storm Targets East," *Wall Street Journal*, October 29, 2012, http://www.wsj.com/articles/SB10001424052970203880704578084502987456668.

12. "Hurricane Sandy Ready to Lash N.J. with Unprecedented Fury," *New Jersey Star Ledger*, October 29, 2012, http://www.nj.com/news/index.ssf/2012/10/nj_braces_for_hurricane_sandy.html.

13. Doyle Rice, "What's in a Name? Frankenstorm vs. Sandy," *USA Today*, October 26, 2012, http://www.usatoday.com/story/weather/2012/10/26/frankenstorm-hurricane-sandy-name/1660867/.

14. "How Sandy Was Dubbed Frankenstorm," *CNN.com*, October 26, 2012, http://news.blogs.cnn.com/2012/10/26/how-sandy-was-dubbed-frankenstorm/.

15. Linda Gonzalez, interview by Trudi-Ann Lawrence, March 20, 2013, Staring Out to Sea: Hurricane Sandy Oral History Project, Louie B. Nunn Center for Oral History, University of Kentucky Libraries, Lexington, https://kentuckyoralhistory.org/ark:/16417/xt77sq8qfp93.

16. Linda Gonzalez interview, March 20, 2013.

17. William Gelhaus, interview by Trudi-Ann Lawrence, September 4, 2013, Staring Out to Sea: Hurricane Sandy Oral History Project, Louie B. Nunn Center for Oral History, University of Kentucky Libraries, Lexington, https://kentuckyoralhistory.org/ark:/16417/xt7h707wq047.

18. Gelhaus interview, September 4, 2013.

19. Keansburg Amusement Park, "History," http://keansburgamusementpark.com/history/, accessed October 5, 2015.

20. Mark Di Ionno, "Keansburg Provides Old-Fashioned Fun Every Summer at NJ's Oldest Amusement Park," *New Jersey Star Ledger*, July 12, 2010, http://blog.nj.com/njv_mark_diionno/2010/07/njs_oldest_amusement_park_brin.html.

21. Di Ionno, "Keansburg Provides."

22. Susan K. Livio, "Keansburg Amusement Park Vows to Rebuild after Hurricane Sandy Destruction," *New Jersey Star Ledger*, November 1, 2012, http://www.nj.com/monmouth/index.ssf/2012/11/keansburg_amusement_park_vows_to_rebuild_after_hurricane_sandy_destruction.html.

23. Di Ionno, "Keansburg Provides."

24. Livio, "Keansburg Amusement Park."

25. Di Ionno, "Keansburg Provides."

26. Diane Bates, *Superstorm Sandy: The Inevitable Destruction and Reconstruction of the Jersey Shore* (New Brunswick, NJ: Rutgers University Press, 2016), 99. The Bayshore is also home to a sizeable population of retirees; in 2012, 28.2 percent of Union Beach residents collected Social Security. The official number of towns along the Bayshore is up for some debate. The New Jersey Chamber of Commerce lists seventeen towns. The 2005 Bayshore Strategic Plan includes only nine municipalities. Monmouth County Planning Board, "Bayshore Region Strategic Plan," September 18, 2006, 2015, https://www.keyportonline.com/filestorage/4031/4646/4243/7119/24-Bayshore_Region_Plan.pdf. Copy in author's possession.

27. US Census Bureau, "Profile of General Population and Housing Characteristics," 2010, https://data.census.gov/cedsci/, accessed November 29, 2021.

28. Bates, *Superstorm Sandy*, 30.

29. As the sociologist Diane Bates noted, European settlement followed the transportation and social networks of the Lenni-Lenape. "Europeans," she wrote, "made use of the Lenape trails and settlement sites, even while gradually eliminating the native populations through land purchases, disease, violence, and eventually, forced displacement." Bates, *Superstorm Sandy*, 31.

30. Randall Gabrielan, *Images of America: Keansburg* (Dover, NH: Arcadia, 1997), 7.

31. Jack Jeandron, *Keyport: From Plantation to Center of Commerce and Industry* (Dover, NH: Arcadia, 2003), 11–15.

32. Timothy Regan, *Images of America: Keyport, New Jersey* (Dover, NH: Arcadia, 1997), 1–27.

33. William Burket, *Images of America: Union Beach* (Dover, NH: Arcadia, 1998), 19; Maxine Lurie and Marc Mappen, eds., *Encyclopedia of New Jersey* (New Brunswick, NJ: Rutgers University Press, 2004), 823, s.v. "Union Beach."

34. New Jersey Home Rule Act, N.J.S.A. 40:42 (1917).

35. The number dropped to 565 when Princeton Borough and Princeton Township merged to become Princeton on January 1, 2013.

36. Bates, *Superstorm Sandy*, 95. For more on the effects of the Home Rule Charter during and after Hurricane Sandy, see chapter 5.

37. Lurie and Mappen, *Encyclopedia of New Jersey*, 306, s.v. "Garden State Parkway."

38. By 2000, the New Jersey Turnpike was the most active nonstop toll road in the nation. Lurie and Mappen, *Encyclopedia of New Jersey*, 579, s.v. "New Jersey Turnpike."

39. Larry Savadova, Margaret Thomas Buchholz, and Bill Bradley, *Great Storms of the Jersey Shore* (West Creek, NJ: Down the Shore, 1997).

40. Robert Pulsch, interview by Brittany Le Strange, May 16, 2013, Staring Out to Sea: Hurricane Sandy Oral History Project, Louie B. Nunn Center for Oral History, University of Kentucky Libraries, Lexington, https://kentuckyoralhistory.org/ark:/16417/xt7rn872z89w.

41. Gabrielan, *Keansburg, New Jersey*, 41.

42. By 2005, Keansburg had pulled lifeguards from the beaches altogether. Monmouth County Planning Board, "Bayshore Region Strategic Plan."

43. Marc Mappen, *There's More to New Jersey Than the Sopranos* (New Brunswick, NJ: Rutgers University Press, 2009), 2.

44. Bates, *Superstorm* Sandy, 28–44.

45. US Census Bureau, "2011 American Community Survey," https://data.census.gov/cedsci/, accessed November 29, 2021.

46. Monmouth County Planning Board, "Bayshore Region Strategic Plan."

47. Monmouth County Planning Board, "Bayshore Region Strategic Plan."

48. Jennifer Rubin, "Christie's Moment: 'Get the Hell off the Beach,'" *Washington Post*, August 29, 2011, http://www.washingtonpost.com/blogs/right-turn/post/christies-moment-get-the-hell-off-the-beach/2011/03/29/gIQANbbQlJ_blog.html.

49. National Oceanic and Atmospheric Administration, "Service Assessment: Hurricane Irene, August 21–30, 2011" (Washington, DC: US Department of Commerce, September 2012), x, https://www.weather.gov/media/publications/assessments/Irene2012.pdf. Copy in author's possession.

50. National Oceanic and Atmospheric Administration, "Service Assessment: Hurricane Irene"; Bates, *Superstorm Sandy*, 123.

51. Adam Bixby, interview by Brittany Le Strange, March 5, 2013, Staring Out to Sea: Hurricane Sandy Oral History Project, Louie B. Nunn Center for Oral History, University of Kentucky Libraries, Lexington, https://kentuckyoralhistory.org/ark:/16417/xt7mgq6r256b.

52. Millie Gonzalez, interview by Trudi-Ann Lawrence, June 12, 2013, Staring Out to Sea: Hurricane Sandy Oral History Project, Louie B. Nunn Center for Oral History, University of Kentucky Libraries, Lexington, https://kentuckyoralhistory.org/ark:/16417/xt7cfx73xr28.

53. Sobel, *Storm Surge*, 136.

54. Kennedy interview, December 16, 2013.

55. Glenn Perroth, interview by Arij Syed, March 25, 2013, Staring Out to Sea: Hurricane Sandy Oral History Project, Louie B. Nunn Center for Oral History, University of Kentucky Libraries, Lexington, https://kentuckyoralhistory.org/ark:/16417/xt78kp7tqf43.

56. Anthony Cavallo, interview by Trudi-Ann Lawrence, August 20, 2013, Staring Out to Sea: Hurricane Sandy Oral History Project, Louie B. Nunn Center for Oral History, University of Kentucky Libraries, Lexington, https://kentuckyoralhistory.org/ark:/16417/xt7tqj77wv52.

57. Sharon Kelly, interview by Trudi-Ann Lawrence, September 4, 2013, Staring Out to Sea: Hurricane Sandy Oral History Project, Louie B. Nunn Center for Oral History, University of Kentucky Libraries, Lexington, https://kentuckyoralhistory.org/ark:/16417/xt7vhh6c5k6h.

58. Miles, *Superstorm*, 159.

59. "How Sandy Was Dubbed Frankenstorm."

60. Miles, *Superstorm*, 221.

61. Miles, *Superstorm*, 221–22.

62. Jenny Portnoy, "With Hurricane Sandy Looming, Christie Tells New Jerseyans to be Smart," *New Jersey Star Ledger*, October 27, 2012, http://www.nj.com/news/index.ssf/2012/10/with_sandy_looming_christie_te.html; Miles, *Superstorm*, 248–49. By declaring a state of emergency, Christie effectively centralized power at the state level. The declaration authorized him to direct resources and personnel to areas in need to aid in rescue, recovery, shelter, essential services, and evacuation. It also enabled him to request federal assistance once the scope of the storm exceeded the state's capacity to respond. New Jersey Office of Emergency Management, New Jersey Department of Law and Public Safety, "Guide to Hurricane Preparedness," http://www.state.nj.us/njoem/soe_faq.html, accessed October 5, 2015.

63. Portnoy, "With Hurricane Sandy Looming."

64. Miles, *Superstorm*, 258.

65. Miles, *Superstorm*, 261.

66. Miles, *Superstorm*, 284–85.

67. Miles, *Superstorm*, 285.

68. Gary Szatkowki, "Very Dangerous Hurricane Sandy: October 28–31, 2012" (Philadelphia; Mount Holly, NJ: National Weather Service, October 28, 2012), http://www.co.hunterdon.nj.us/911/oem/Sandy2012/NWS-Briefings/8Oct28-12noon.pdf; also cited by Miles, *Superstorm*, 285–86; Sobel, *Storm Surge*, 136–37; Kate Bilo, "National Weather Service: Sandy a 'Very Dangerous Storm,'" Philadelphia CBS Local, October 28, 2012, https://philadelphia.cbslocal.com/2012/10/28/the-national-weather-service-statement-sandy-a-very-dangerous-storm/.

69. The National Weather Service defines a surge as an abnormal sea level accompanying a hurricane or other intense storm. The height of a surge is the difference between the observed level of the sea surface and the level that would have occurred in the absence of the cyclone. National Oceanic and Atmospheric Administration, "Service Assessment: Hurricane/Post-Tropical Cyclone Sandy, October 22–29, 2012" (Washington, DC: United States Department of Commerce, May 2013), https://www.weather.gov/media/publications/assessments/Sandy13.pdf. Copy in author's possession.

70. Miles, *Superstorm*, 307.

71. Scott Gurian, "After Sandy, One Business Owner Picks Up the Pieces," *New Jersey News*, November 12, 2012, http://www.wnyc.org/story/251963-after-sandy-one-business-owner-picks-pieces-pitching/.

72. Angelita Dorr, interview by Brittany Le Strange, March 22, 2013, Staring Out to Sea: Hurricane Sandy Oral History Project, Louie B. Nunn Center for Oral History, University of Kentucky Libraries, Lexington, https://kentuckyoralhistory.org/ark:/16417/xt7j6q1sj53b.

73. Dorr interview, March 22, 2013.

74. Wolf Blitzer, *The Situation Room*, CNN, transcript, October 29, 2012, http://www.cnn.com/TRANSCRIPTS/1210/29/sitroom.02.html.

75. "Governor Christie Chastises Atlantic City Mayor," *USA Today*, October 30, 2012, http://www.usatoday.com/story/weather/2012/10/29/taking-no-chances-in-atlantic-city/1667771/; Miles, *Superstorm*, 316–17; Blitzer, *The Situation Room*, October 29, 2012.

76. Michael Melfi, interview by Mary Piasecki, September 24, 2013, Staring Out to Sea: Hurricane Sandy Oral History Project, Louie B. Nunn Center for Oral History, University of Kentucky Libraries, Lexington, https://kentuckyoralhistory.org/ark:/16417/xt7x959c8h02.

77. Miles, *Superstorm*, 320–21.

78. Christina Ng, "Superstorm Sandy Crashes Ashore in New Jersey," *ABC News*, October 29, 2012, http://abcnews.go.com/US/hurricane-sandy-makes-landfall-jersey/story?id=17592795.

79. "Hurricane Sandy Makes Landfall near Atlantic City," *New Jersey Star Ledger*, October 29, 2012, http://www.nj.com/news/index.ssf/2012/10/hurricane_sandy_makes_landfall.html.

80. Michael Melfi interview, September 24, 2013.

## 2. "PLEASE, SANDY, NO MORE"

1. Mary Jane Michalak and Roger Michalak, interview by Trudi-Ann Lawrence, October 23, 2013, Staring Out to Sea: Hurricane Sandy Oral History Project, Louie B. Nunn Center for Oral History, University of Kentucky Libraries, Lexington, https://kentuckyoralhistory.org/ark:/16417/xt7sj38kh78v.

2. Mary Jane Michalak and Roger Michalak interview, October 23, 2013.

3. Mary Jane Michalak and Roger Michalak interview, October 23, 2013.

4. Sobel, *Storm Surge*, 150.

5. Sobel, *Storm Surge*, 145.

6. Joseph Bilinski et al., "Damage Assessment Report on the Effects of Hurricane Sandy on the State of New Jersey's Natural Resources" (Trenton: Office of Science, New Jersey Department of Environmental Protection, May 2015), 8, https://www.nj.gov/dep/dsr/publications/hurricane-sandy-assessment.pdf.

7. Sobel, *Storm Surge*, 140–41.

8. Linda Gonzalez interview, March 20, 2013.

9. Linda Gonzalez interview, March 20, 2013.

10. Linda Gonzalez, "New Jersey Strong," 2012. Poem in Trudi-Ann Lawrence's possession.

11. Linda Gonzalez interview, March 20, 2013.

12. Andrea Bulvid, interview by Trudi-Ann Lawrence, June 5, 2013, Staring Out to Sea: Hurricane Sandy Oral History Project, Louie B. Nunn Center for Oral History, University of Kentucky Libraries, Lexington, https://kentuckyoralhistory.org/ark:/16417/xt734t-6f4h1w.

13. Bulvid interview, June 5, 2013.

14. Bulvid interview, June 5, 2013.

15. Bulvid interview, June 5, 2013.

16. Bulvid interview, June 5, 2013.

17. Bulvid interview, June 5, 2013.

18. Andrea Bulvid, photograph, October 29, 2012. Screenshot pulled from Bulvid's Facebook feed by author, with Bulvid's permission.

19. Kennedy interview, December 16, 2013.

20. Kennedy interview, December 16, 2013.

21. Kennedy interview, December 16, 2013.

22. Joann Melfi and Michael Melfi, interview by Mary Piasecki, September 24, 2013, Staring Out to Sea: Hurricane Sandy Oral History Project, Louie B. Nunn Center for Oral History, University of Kentucky Libraries, Lexington, https://kentuckyoralhistory.org/ark:/16417/xt7x959c8h02.

23. Joann Melfi and Michael Melfi interview, September 24, 2013.

24. Cheryl Mara, interview by Trudi-Ann Lawrence, August 26, 2013, Staring Out to Sea: Hurricane Sandy Oral History Project, Louie B. Nunn Center for Oral History, University of Kentucky Libraries, Lexington, https://kentuckyoralhistory.org/ark:/16417/xt75tb0xsc0g.

25. Mara interview, August 26, 2013.

26. Mara interview, August 26, 2013.

27. Dorr interview, March 22, 2013.

28. Dorr interview, March 22, 2013.

29. Dorr interview, March 22, 2013.

30. Mary Jane and Roger Michalak interview, October 23, 2013.

31. Livio, "Keansburg Amusement Park"; Kelly Jane Cotter, "Founded in 1904, Keansburg Amusement Park Still Charms, *Asbury Park Press*, August 20, 2014, http://www.app.com/story/entertainment/events/2014/08/20/founded-keansburg-amusement-park-still-charms/14343591/.

32. Millie Gonzalez interview, June 12, 2013.

33. Sarah E. Griesemer, "Iconic Restaurant Finally Reopens after Sandy," *Asbury Park Press*, August 26, 2015, http://www.app.com/story/entertainment/dining/2015/08/26/old-heidelberg-inn-reopens/32404121/.

34. Millie Gonzalez interview, June 12, 2013.

35. Millie Gonzalez interview, June 12, 2013.

36. Linda Gonzalez interview, March 20, 2013.

37. Linda Gonzalez interview, March 20, 2013.

38. James Butler, interview by Trudi-Ann Lawrence, July 11, 2013, Staring Out to Sea: Hurricane Sandy Oral History Project, Louie B. Nunn Center for Oral History, University of Kentucky Libraries, Lexington, https://kentuckyoralhistory.org/ark:/16417/xt7zgm81p36h.

39. Butler interview, July 11, 2013.

40. Butler interview, July 11, 2013.

41. Butler interview, July 11, 2013.

## 3. "EVERYTHING IS GONE"

1. Anthony Cavallo interview, August 20, 2013.

2. Anthony Cavallo interview, August 20, 2013.

3. Anthony Cavallo interview, August 20, 2013.

4. Anthony Cavallo interview, August 20, 2013.

5. Anthony Cavallo interview, August 20, 2013.

6. Anthony Cavallo interview, August 20, 2013.

7. "Raritan Bay and Sandy Hook Bay, New Jersey, Limited Reevaluation Report for Coastal Storm Risk Management, Union Beach New Jersey" (New York: US Army Corps of Engineers, New York District, September 2016), https://www.nan.usace.army.mil/Portals/37/docs/civilworks/projects/nj/coast/UNBE/AppendixBEconomics.pdf?ver=2016-10-03-122315-957; Eugene Paik, "Six Months after Sandy, Union Beach Begins to Come Back to Life," New Jersey Star Ledger, April 28, 2013, http://www.nj.com/monmouth/index.ssf/2013/04/union_beach_rebuilding_plods_along_6_months_after_sandy.html.

8. Molly Hennessy-Fiske, "For Small Township's Police Chief, Sandy's Destruction Hits Home," Los Angeles Times, October 31, 2012, https://www.latimes.com/nation/la-xpm-2012-oct-31-la-na-nn-new-jersey-union-beach-homes-20121031-story.html.

9. Millie Gonzalez interview, June 12, 2013.

10. Bulvid interview, June 5, 2013.

11. Bulvid interview, June 5, 2013.

12. Anthony Cavallo interview, August 20, 2013.

13. Anthony Cavallo interview, August 20, 2013.

14. Linda Gonzalez interview, March 20, 2013.

15. Iris Miranda, interview by Trudi-Ann Lawrence, May 15, 2013, Staring Out to Sea: Hurricane Sandy Oral History Project, Louie B. Nunn Center for Oral History, University of Kentucky Libraries, Lexington, https://kentuckyoralhistory.org/ark:/16417/xt7n-vx06165c.

16. Henrietta Williams, interview by Trudi-Ann Lawrence, September 3, 2013, Staring Out to Sea: Hurricane Sandy Oral History Project, Louie B. Nunn Center for Oral History, University of Kentucky Libraries, Lexington, https://kentuckyoralhistory.org/ark:/16417/xt76m902233j.

17. Williams interview, September 3, 2013.

18. According to the US Energy Information Administration, on November 2, 67 percent of stations in the New York City metro area were without gasoline. "Hurricane Sandy Situation Report" (Washington, DC: US Department of Energy, November 4, 2012), https://www.energy.gov/sites/prod/files/2012_SitRep15_Sandy_11042012_300PM%20.pdf.

19. Bulvid interview, June 5, 2013.

20. Anthony Cavallo interview, August 20, 2013. There were no reports of widespread looting in the wake of Hurricane Sandy, but residents reported isolated instances throughout

the state. According to the Monmouth County prosecutor, in the first three weeks after the storm, there were twenty-five arrests. Amy Lieberman, "Hurricane Sandy's Dark Side: Looting and Other Crime," *Christian Science Monitor*, November 3, 2012, https://www.csmoni tor.com/USA/2012/1103/Hurricane-Sandy-s-darker-side-Looting-and-other-crime.

21. Butler interview, July 11, 2013.

22. In the 1912 election, the Democratic nominee, Woodrow Wilson, garnered 48.6 percent of the vote; Teddy Roosevelt, running on the Progressive ticket, earned 33.2 percent.

23. Bixby interview, March 5, 2013.

24. Bulvid interview, June 5, 2013.

25. Pulsch interview, May 16, 2013.

26. Matt Katz, *American Governor: Chris Christie's Bridge to Redemption* (New York: Threshold Editions, 2016) 186.

27. Linda Gonzalez interview, March 20, 2013.

28. Bixby interview, March 5, 2013.

29. Maureen Piasecki and John Piasecki, interview by Alicia Hill, March 25, 2013, Staring Out to Sea: Hurricane Sandy Oral History Project, Louie B. Nunn Center for Oral History, University of Kentucky Libraries, Lexington, https://kentuckyoralhistory.org/ark:/16417/xt712j685x6s.

30. Kathleen O'Halleran, interview by Brittany Le Strange, June 19, 2013, Staring Out to Sea: Hurricane Sandy Oral History Project, Louie B. Nunn Center for Oral History, University of Kentucky Libraries, Lexington, https://kentuckyoralhistory.org/ark:/16417/xt7dbr8mgq17.

31. "The Governor, The President, and Sandy: Good Numbers in the Days after the Storm," press release (Teaneck, NJ: Fairleigh Dickinson University, November 26, 2012), accessed October 20, 2017, http://publicmind.fdu.edu/2012/goodnumbers/.

32. Katz, *American Governor*, 186.

33. Katz, *American Governor*, 192–93.

34. Kelly interview, September 4, 2013. A week later, Christie issued a directive authorizing displaced New Jersey residents to vote through email and fax; those showing up to vote in person could do so at any polling location throughout the state. On November 6, 58 percent of New Jersey voters elected Obama to a second term in office. In Monmouth County, Romney won by a 5.5-point margin. "2012 New Jersey Presidential Results," *Politico*, November 19, 2012, https://www.politico.com/2012-election/results/president/new-jersey/.

35. Butler interview, July 11, 2013.

36. Mara interview, August 26, 2013.

37. Perroth interview, March 25, 2013.

38. Linda Gonzalez interview, March 20, 2013.

39. Mara interview, August 26, 2013.

40. Joann Melfi and Michael Melfi interview, September 24, 2013.

41. Linda Gonzalez interview, March 20, 2013.

42. Linda Gonzalez interview, March 20, 2013.

43. Mara interview, August 26, 2013.

44. Sal Cortale, interview by Brittany Le Strange, June 19, 2013, Staring Out to Sea: Hurricane Sandy Oral History Project, Louie B. Nunn Center for Oral History, University of Kentucky Libraries, Lexington, https://kentuckyoralhistory.org/ark:/16417/xt7pzg6g4m08.

45. Anthony Cavallo interview, August 20, 2013.

46. Joann Melfi, interview by Mary Piasecki, September 24, 2013, Staring Out to Sea: Hurricane Sandy Oral History Project, Louie B. Nunn Center for Oral History,

University of Kentucky Libraries, Lexington, https://kentuckyoralhistory.org/ark:/16417/xt7x959c8h02.

47. Millie Gonzalez interview, June 12, 2013.

48. Millie Gonzalez interview, June 12, 2013.

49. Ashley Peskoe, "Iconic Hurricane Sandy Image Still Brings Pride, Pain to Union Beach Man," *New Jersey Star Ledger*, October 23, 2013, http://www.nj.com/monmouth/index.ssf/2013/10/iconic_hurricane_sandy_image_still_brings_pride_pain_to_union_beach_man.html.

50. Bulvid interview, June 5, 2013.

51. Millie Gonzalez interview, June 12, 2013.

52. Butler interview, July 11, 2013.

53. Miranda interview, May 15, 2013.

54. Michael Melfi interview, September 24, 2013.

55. Maureen Piasecki, interview by Alicia Hill, March 25, 2013, Staring Out to Sea: Hurricane Sandy Oral History Project, Louie B. Nunn Center for Oral History, University of Kentucky Libraries, Lexington, https://kentuckyoralhistory.org/ark:/16417/xt712j685x6s.

56. Anthony Cavallo interview, August 20, 2013.

57. Anthony Cavallo interview, August 20, 2013.

## 4. "YOU CAN'T WASH AWAY HOPE"

1. Comment on James Butler's Facebook page, November 9, 2012 (12:56 a.m.), https://www.facebook.com/JamesButlerJr. All quotes from Butler's Facebook page are used with his permission.

2. Comment on James Butler's Facebook page, November 9, 2012 (12:56 a.m.).

3. Comment on James Butler's Facebook page, November 9, 2012 (12:56 a.m.).

4. Comment on James Butler's Facebook page, November 9, 2012 (1:31 a.m.).

5. Comment on James Butler's Facebook page, November 9, 2012 (1:45 a.m.).

6. Comment on James Butler's Facebook page, November 9, 2012 (2:03 a.m.).

7. Comment on James Butler's Facebook page, November 9, 2012 (2:05 a.m.).

8. Comment on James Butler's Facebook page, November 9, 2012 (7:55 a.m.).

9. Comment on James Butler's Facebook page, November 9, 2012 (10:47 a.m.).

10. UNION Beach HOPE Tree Facebook page, November 25, 2012, https://www.facebook.com/UNION-Beach-HOPE-Tree-371466136281103/, November 25, 2012.

11. UNION Beach HOPE Tree Facebook page, September 16, 2013; comment on UNION Beach HOPE Tree Facebook page, November 25, 2012 (10:30 a.m.).

12. UNION Beach HOPE Tree Facebook page, March 13, 2013.

13. UNION Beach HOPE Tree Facebook page, March 28, 2013.

14. UB Hope Facebook page, November 25, 2012, https://www.facebook.com/ub.hope.

15. UB Hope Facebook page, November 26, 2012.

16. UB Hope Facebook page, November 25, 2012.

17. In the summer of 2013, the Union Beach Hope Tree was transported down the Garden State Parkway to take its place in a temporary exhibit at the Tuckerton Seaport and Baymen's Museum, developed by three of the students who worked on the Staring Out to Sea Oral History Project. For more on the project, see appendix B.

18. UB Hope Facebook page, November 25, 2012.

19. UB Hope Facebook page, November 25, 2012; comment on UNION Beach HOPE Tree Facebook page, November 25, 2012 (10:30 a.m.).

20. UNION Beach HOPE Tree Facebook page, November 24, 2012; comment on UNION Beach HOPE Tree Facebook page, November 24, 2012 (8:45 a.m.); comment on

UNION Beach HOPE Tree Facebook page, November 25 (11:08 p.m.); comment on UB Hope Facebook page, December 14, 2012 (12:27 a.m.). Waterproof signs were donated by The Sign Maker on Union Avenue.

21. Butler interview, July 11, 2013.

22. Anthony Cavallo interview, August 20, 2013.

23. Butler interview, July 11, 2013; UNION Beach HOPE Tree Facebook page, December 1, 2012.

24. Comment on UNION Beach HOPE Tree Facebook page, December 1, 2012 (3:45 p.m.).

25. Comment on UNION Beach HOPE Tree Facebook page, December 2, 2012 (7:13 p.m.).

26. UNION Beach HOPE Tree Facebook page, December 4, 2012; UNION Beach HOPE Tree Facebook page, December 5, 2012.

27. UNION Beach HOPE Tree Facebook page, December 15, 2012; comment on UNION Beach HOPE Tree Facebook page, December 15, 2012 (7:01 p.m.); comment on UNION Beach HOPE Tree Facebook page, December 15, 2012 (7:03 p.m.).

28. Comment on UNION Beach HOPE Tree Facebook page, December 15, 2012 (7:07 p.m.); comment on UNION Beach HOPE Tree Facebook page, December 15, 2012 (7:08 p.m.).

29. Comment on UNION Beach HOPE Tree Facebook page, December 15, 2012 (7:07 p.m.); Comments on UNION Beach HOPE Tree Facebook page, December 15, 2012 (9:19 p.m.) through December 16, 2012 (8:20 p.m.).

30. Comment on UNION Beach HOPE Tree Facebook page, December 15, 2012 (6:38 p.m.); Comment on UNION Beach HOPE Tree Facebook page, December 17, 2012 (5:42 p.m.).

31. UNION Beach HOPE Tree Facebook page, December 24, 2012; comment on UNION Beach HOPE Tree Facebook page, December 19, 2012 (4:06 p.m.); comment on UNION Beach HOPE Tree Facebook page, December 15, 2012 (7:03 p.m.); comment on UNION Beach HOPE Tree Facebook page, December 15, 2012 (1:53 p.m.).

32. UNION Beach HOPE Tree Facebook page, February 23, 2013.

33. UNION Beach HOPE Tree Facebook page, March 29, 2013; comment on UNION Beach HOPE Tree Facebook page, March 30, 2013 (9:30 a.m.).

34. Some in New Jersey blamed the state's home rule system for the inefficient and uneven disbursement of funds. In 2012, the state was home to 566 independent municipalities. Within its borders, the state supported 611 public school districts, more than 500 mayors and police chiefs, and hundreds of water departments, tax-collection agencies, and emergency services. In the immediate aftermath of Sandy, critics argued that the home rule system was responsible for inefficiency and high costs, which were the result of unnecessary duplication of services and high-level administrative positions. None of our oral history narrators were among these critics in our interviews with them, and in reality, New Jersey's municipal system likely had little effect on the short-term disbursement of relief. As the political scientist Stephanie Hoopes Halpin wrote, "There is nothing extraordinary about New Jersey's municipal laws, size or number of towns that would make their response to disaster unique or exceptional. Nor would it prevent their municipal response activities from being compared to municipalities across the country." Stephanie Hoopes Halpin, "Home Rule in NJ and Hurricane Sandy Recovery: Managing Power Restoration, Gas Rationing, Debris Removal, and Temporary Housing" (paper presented at the American Society for Public Administration annual conference, May 2013); Sarah Watson, "Hurricane Sandy Revealed the Pluses and Minuses of Home Rule," *Press of Atlantic City*, December 2, 2013, http://www.pressofatlanticcity.com/news/press/ocean/hurricane-sandy-revealed-the-pluses-and-minuses-of-home-rule/article_94332030-5b0c-11e3-b398-0019bb2963f4.html;

35. Carol Chang, chief programs officer, North Jersey Region, American Red Cross, cited by Stephanie Hoopes Halpin, "Non-Profit Groups in Superstorm Sandy: Local Surge Capacity or Long-Term Recovery?" (paper presented at the forty-second annual conference of the Association for Research on Nonprofit Organization and Voluntary Action, Hartford, CT, November 2013); Pam Fessler, "Thanks, But No Thanks: When Post-Disaster Donations Overwhelm," *NPR.org*, January 9, 2013, http://www.npr.org/2013/01/09/168946170/thanks-but-no-thanks-when-post-disasterdonations-over whelm.

36. Halpin, "Non-Profit Groups in Superstorm Sandy."

37. Collette Kennedy, interview by author, May 28, 2015, Staring Out to Sea: Hurricane Sandy Oral History Project, Louie B. Nunn Center for Oral History, University of Kentucky Libraries, Lexington, https://kentuckyoralhistory.org/ark:/16417/xt7g7940vt8c.

38. Kennedy interview, December 16, 2013.

39. Kennedy interview, December 16, 2013. This is common practice at disaster shelters. Although the Keyport shelter was run independently, it adhered to the same standards and protocol established by the Red Cross for shelter situations.

40. Kennedy interview, December 16, 2013.

41. Cortale interview, June 19, 2013.

42. Cortale interview, June 19, 2013.

43. Cortale interview, June 19, 2013.

44. O'Halleran interview, June 19, 2013.

45. Christina Leslie, "Storm-Ravaged Project PAUL Reopens Its Doors," *Monitor*, April 11, 2013, http://www.trentonmonitor.com/main.asp?SectionID=4&SubSectionID= 140&ArticleID=5076.

46. Because St. Anne's Roman Catholic Church owns the building where Project PAUL is housed, the project was covered by the Diocese of Trenton's insurance. The diocese covers parishes throughout the state and was quick to respond to the claims Cortale filed. In total, fifty-one sites under the policy—retreat houses, convents, rectories, and schools—incurred storm-related damage.

47. Cortale interview, June 19, 2013.

48. Leslie, "Storm-Ravaged Project PAUL Reopens Its Doors."

49. Carl Williamson, interview by Grace Jeong, Hurricane Sandy Oral History Project, April 14, 2015, College of New Jersey, Ewing, https://hurricanesandy.pages.tcnj.edu/2015/05/13/a-preacher-and-a-bar-owner/.

50. Gigi Liaguno-Dorr [Angelita Dorr], interview by Grace Jeong, Hurricane Sandy Oral History Project, April 14, 2015, College of New Jersey, Ewing, https://hurricane-sandy.pages.tcnj.edu/2015/05/19/we-think-we-can-we-did/; Bobby Ross, Jr., "New Jersey Congregation Brings Hope to Beach Town Hit Hard by Superstorm Sandy," *Christian Chronicle*, November 3, 2012, https://christianchronicle.org/new-jersey-congregation-brings-hope-to-beach-town-hit-hard-by-superstorm-sandy/.

51. Dorr interview, March 22, 2013.

52. Dorr interview, March 22, 2013.

53. Dorr interview, April 14, 2015.

54. Dorothy Gajewski, interview by Trudi-Ann Lawrence, August 28, 2013, Staring Out to Sea: Hurricane Sandy Oral History Project, Louie B. Nunn Center for Oral History, University of Kentucky Libraries, Lexington, https://kentuckyoralhistory.org/ark:/16417/xt7n028pg78x.

55. Karen Kiely, interview by Trudi-Ann Lawrence, December 6, 2013, Staring Out to Sea: Hurricane Sandy Oral History Project, Louie B. Nunn Center for Oral History, University of Kentucky Libraries, Lexington, https://kentuckyoralhistory.org/ark:/16417/xt7bk35mcs3q.

56. Dorr interview, March 22, 2013; Carl Williamson, interview by Grace Jeong, Hurricane Sandy Oral History Project, April 14, 2015, College of New Jersey, Ewing, https://hurricanesandy.pages.tcnj.edu/2015/05/13/a-preacher-and-a-bar-owner/. There is some discrepancy in the moniker, with Dorr referring to them as the "pastor and the bar owner" and Carl declaring them the "preacher and the bar owner."

57. Williamson interview, April 14, 2015; Ross, "New Jersey Congregation Brings Hope."

58. Dorr interview, March 22, 2013.

59. "A Rabbi and a Pastor Walk into a Bar—and Decide to Rebuild It," *PRWeb.com*, August 1, 2013, http://www.prweb.com/releases/jakeabobs/cabinethardware/prweb10918492.htm.

60. The sign ended up on the door of the original Jakeabob's in November 2012. Comment on UNION Beach HOPE Tree Facebook page, November 25, 2012 (8:45 a.m.). The sign was moved to the Off the Bay location when it opened.

61. "A Rabbi and a Pastor Walk into a Bar."

62. Paper Doors for Gigi was organized as a Facebook event in February 2013; Jakeabob's also posted a picture of its new menu when it reopened in April 2013.

## 5. A MODEL OF DISASTER PREPAREDNESS

1. Bixby interview, March 5, 2013.

2. Bixby interview, March 5, 2013.

3. Hank Kalet, "Renters: Hurricane Sandy's Invisible Victims," *NJ Spotlight*, June 26, 2013, http://www.njspotlight.com/stories/13/06/25/renters-hurricane-sandy-s-invisible-victims/.

4. Insurance Information Institute, "Facts and Statistics: Flood Insurance," https://www.iii.org/fact-statistic/facts-statistics-flood-insurance, accessed July 20, 2018.

5. Adam Bixby, interview by Ruqayyah Abdullah, May 15, 2015, Staring Out to Sea: Hurricane Sandy Oral History Project, Louie B. Nunn Center for Oral History, University of Kentucky Libraries, Lexington, https://kentuckyoralhistory.org/ark:/16417/xt7gqn-5z8x0z.

6. Bixby interview, March 5, 2013; Bixby interview, May 15, 2015.

7. Bixby interview, May 15, 2015.

8. Dorr interview, March 22, 2013.

9. Anthony Cavallo interview, August 20, 2013.

10. Robert Gajewski, interview by Trudi-Ann Lawrence, August 28, 2013, Staring Out to Sea: Hurricane Sandy Oral History Project, Louie B. Nunn Center for Oral History, University of Kentucky Libraries, Lexington, https://kentuckyoralhistory.org/ark:/16417/xt7n028pg78x.

11. Dorothy Gajewski interview, August 28, 2013.

12. Dorothy Gajewski and Robert Gajewski, interview by Trudi-Ann Lawrence, August 28, 2013, Staring Out to Sea: Hurricane Sandy Oral History Project, Louie B. Nunn Center for Oral History, University of Kentucky Libraries, Lexington, https://kentuckyoralhistory.org/ark:/16417/xt7n028pg78x.

13. Christopher Cooper and Robert Block, *Disaster: Hurricane Katrina and the Failure of Homeland Security* (New York: Holt Paperbacks, 2007), 47.

14. Cooper and Block, *Disaster*, 47.

15. Cooper and Block, *Disaster*, 49.

16. Cooper and Block, *Disaster*, 50.

17. Cooper and Block, *Disaster*, 52.

18. Cooper and Block, *Disaster*, 55.

19. For more on the political impact of Hurricane Andrew, see David Twigg, *The Politics of Disaster: Tracking the Impact of Hurricane Andrew* (Gainesville: University Press of Florida, 2012).

20. Cooper and Block, *Disaster*, 58–59.

21. Edward Walsh, "It Took a County Judge to Bail Out FEMA," *Washington Post*, April 19, 1998, https://www.washingtonpost.com/archive/politics/1998/08/19/it-took-a-county-judge-to-bail-out-fema/44c64f30-e58a-4abf-9654-72898b63bad7/.

22. Walsh, "It Took a County Judge."

23. Walsh, "It Took a County Judge."

24. Chris Post, "Making Place through the Memorial Landscape," in Jeffrey Smith, ed., *Explorations in Place Attachment* (New York: Routledge, 2018), 89.

25. Walsh, "It Took a County Judge."

26. Terrorist Research and Analytical Center, National Security Division, "Terrorism in the United States" (Washington, DC: Department of Justice, Federal Bureau of Investigation, 1995), i; excerpt also cited in Cooper and Block, *Disaster*, 65.

27. Cooper and Block, *Disaster*, 65.

28. Michael Melfi interview, September 24, 2013.

29. Michael Melfi interview, September 24, 2013.

30. Michael Melfi interview, September 24, 2013.

31. Miranda interview, May 15, 2013.

32. Miranda interview, May 15, 2013.

33. Miranda interview, May 15, 2013.

34. Bixby interview, March 5, 2013.

35. "A Homeowner's Guide to Retrofitting: Six Ways to Protect Your Home from Flooding," third edition (Washington, DC: Federal Emergency Management Agency, June 2014), 87.

36. Bixby interview, May 15, 2015.

37. Perroth interview, March 25, 2013.

38. Cortale interview, June 19, 2013.

39. Jane Jacobs, *The Death and Life of Great American Cities* (New York: Random House, 1961), 35.

40. Bixby interview, May 15, 2015.

41. Federal Emergency Management Agency, "Fact Sheet: Increased Cost of Compliance Coverage," https://www.fema.gov/sites/default/files/2020-08/fema_increased-cost-of-compliance_fact-sheet.pdf, accessed October 25, 2021. Copy in author's possession.

42. Bixby interview, May 15, 2015.

43. Bixby interview, May 15, 2015.

44. Dorothy Gajewski and Robert Gajewski interview, August 28, 2013.

45. Millie Gonzalez interview, June 12, 2013.

46. Millie Gonzalez interview, June 12, 2013.

47. Mark Murray, "FEMA Director Has a Tough Act to Follow," *Government Executive*, June 5, 2001, https://www.govexec.com/management/2001/06/fema-director-has-a-tough-act-to-follow/9260/.

48. Scott Knowles, "Learning from Disaster? The History of Technology and the Future of Disaster Research," *Technology and Culture* 55, no. 4 (October 2014): 776; Scott Knowles, *Disaster Experts: Mastering Risk in Modern America* (Philadelphia: University of Pennsylvania Press, 2012), 17.

49. Knowles, *Disaster Experts*, 69–70.

50. Knowles, *Disaster Experts*, 70.

51. Knowles, *Disaster Experts*, 72.

52. Cooper and Block, *Disaster*, 73.

53. Knowles, *Disaster Experts*, 75.

54. Knowles, *Disaster Experts*, 286–87.

55. Eugene Provenzo and Asterie Baker Provenzo, *In the Eye of Hurricane Andrew* (Gainesville: University Press of Florida, 2002), 8.

56. "Hurricane Pam Exercise Concludes," press release (Washington, DC: Federal Emergency Management Agency, July 23, 2014). Copy in author's possession.

57. William Freudenberg et al., *Catastrophe in the Making: The Engineering of Katrina* (Washington, DC: Island, 2011), 21.

58. Freudenberg et al., *Catastrophe in the Making*, 21.

59. Bixby interview, May 15, 2015.

60. Michael Melfi interview, September 24, 2013.

61. Roger Michalak, interview by Trudi-Ann Lawrence, October 23, 2013, Staring Out to Sea: Hurricane Sandy Oral History Project, Louie B. Nunn Center for Oral History, University of Kentucky Libraries, Lexington, https://kentuckyoralhistory.org/ark:/16417/xt7sj38kh78v.

62. Anthony Cavallo interview, August 20, 2013.

63. Anthony Cavallo interview, August 20, 2013.

64. Anthony Cavallo interview, August 20, 2013.

65. Anthony Cavallo interview, August 20, 2013.

66. Anthony Cavallo interview, August 20, 2013.

67. "FEMA Rejects Funding for Nearly 100 Beach Homes Destroyed by Sandy," *CBSNewYork.com*, August 12, 2013, http://newyork.cbslocal.com/2013/08/12/fema-rejecting-funding-for-nearly-100-union-beach-homes-destroyed-in-sandy/.

68. "FEMA Rejects Funding."

69. Anthony Cavallo interview, August 20, 2013.

70. John Piasecki, interview by Alicia Hill, March 25, 2013, Staring Out to Sea: Hurricane Sandy Oral History Project, Louie B. Nunn Center for Oral History, University of Kentucky Libraries, Lexington, https://kentuckyoralhistory.org/ark:/16417/xt712j685x6s.

71. John Piasecki interview, March 25, 2013.

72. "FEMA Rejects Funding."

73. Mary Jane Michalak, interview by Trudi-Ann Lawrence, October 23, 2013, Staring Out to Sea: Hurricane Sandy Oral History Project, Louie B. Nunn Center for Oral History, University of Kentucky Libraries, Lexington, https://kentuckyoralhistory.org/ark:/16417/xt7sj38kh78v.

74. Roger Michalak and Mary Jane Michalak interview, October 23, 2013.

75. Roger Michalak interview, October 23, 2013.

76. Bixby interview, May 15, 2015.

77. Roger Michalak interview, October 23, 2013.

78. "Many Homes Not Yet Rebuilt, Residents Feel Stuck in Union Beach, NJ Two Years after Sandy," *CBSNewYork.com*, October 28, 2014, http://newyork.cbslocal.com/2014/10/28/many-homes-not-yet-rebuilt-residents-feel-stuck-in-union-beach-n-j-2-years-after-sandy/.

79. "Many Homes Not Yet Rebuilt."

80. Anthony Cavallo interview, August 20, 2013.

**6. "THERE IS NO SUCH THING AS A NATURAL DISASTER"**

1. "Thursday: Port Monmouth Flood Project," *NJ Patch*, March 6, 2013, https://patch.com/new-jersey/middletown-nj/an--port-monmouth-flood-project-3cfa4c40.

2. I attended this meeting with several of the students involved in the Staring Out to Sea Oral History Project. For more, see appendix B.

3. John Piasecki interview, March 25, 2013.

4. Michael Melfi interview, September 24, 2013.

5. Joann Melfi interview, September 24, 2013.

6. Pulsch interview, May 16, 2013.

7. Michael Melfi interview, September 24, 2013.

8. "Port Monmouth Flood Project."

9. Perroth interview, March 25, 2013.

10. Miranda interview, May 15, 2013. The "Spy House" refers to the Seabrook-Wilson House, a seaside homestead built in the late seventeenth century. Despite legends of Revolutionary War espionage, evidence indicates that the site was a private residence for much of the two centuries that followed, occupied by prominent Port Monmouth families. It fell into disuse in the 1960s. The Middletown Township Historical Society took over and renovated the property, adding it to the National Register of Historic Places in 1974.

11. Anthony Cavallo interview, August 20, 2013.

12. John Piasecki interview, March 25, 2013.

13. Miranda interview, May 15, 2013.

14. Pulsch interview, May 16, 2013.

15. David Kutner, phone conversation with author, February 10, 2015. Notes in author's possession.

16. National Oceanic and Atmospheric Administration, "National Coastal Population Report" (Washington, DC: Department of Commerce, March 2013), https://aamb publicoceanservice.blob.core.windows.net/oceanserviceprod/facts/coastal-popula tion-report.pdf. File in author's possession. In 2010 an additional 15 percent of the population—40.5 million people—was living in coastal watershed counties, areas in which water and materials are drawn into a bay or ocean.

17. Kutner, phone conversation with author, February 10, 2015. During the twentieth century, New Jersey's four coastal counties, those most at risk for storm damage, experienced a 916 percent population growth, more than double the growth in the state at large. James K. Mitchell, "A Century of Natural Disasters in a State of Changing Vulnerability: New Jersey, 1900–1999," in *New Jersey's Environments: Past, Present, and Future*, ed. Neil Maher (New Brunswick, NJ: Rutgers University Press, 2006), 176.

18. Knowles, *Disaster Experts*, 297.

19. "Restoring the Quality of Our Environment: Report of the Environmental Pollution Panel, President's Science Advisory Committee" (Washington, DC: White House, November 1965), https://dge.carnegiescience.edu/labs/caldeiralab/Caldeira%20down loads/PSAC,%201965,%20Restoring%20the%20Quality%20of%20Our%20Environ ment.pdf.

20. "Third National Climate Assessment" (Washington, DC: US Global Change Research Program, 2014), https://nca2014.globalchange.gov/.

21. Union of Concerned Scientists, "Encroaching Tides: How Sea Level Rise and Tidal Flooding Threaten US East and Gulf Coast Communities over the Next 30 Years," October 2014, https://www.ucsusa.org/sites/default/files/attach/2014/10/encroach ing-tides-full-report.pdf#page=48, citing Claudia Tebaldi et al., "Modeling Sea Level Impacts on Storm Surges along US Coasts," *Environmental Research Letters* 7, no. 1 (2012).

22. Kutner, phone conversation with author, February 10, 2015.

23. Lisa Rose, "50 Years Later, NJ Remembers the Storm That Swallowed the Jersey Shore," *New Jersey Star Ledger*, March 8, 2012, http://www.nj.com/news/index. ssf/2012/03/50_years_later_nj_remembers_wh.html; Emil Salvini, "The Great Atlantic Storm of 1962," *NJ Spotlight News*, March 6, 2012, http://www.njtvonline.org/news/uncate gorized/the-great-atlantic-storm-of-1962/.

24. Rose, "50 Years Later."

25. Kutner, phone conversation with author, February 10, 2015.

26. Kelly interview, September 4, 2013; Sharon Kelly, interview by Ruqayyah Abdullah, May 28, 2015, Staring Out to Sea: Hurricane Sandy Oral History Project, Louie B. Nunn Center for Oral History, University of Kentucky Libraries, Lexington, https://kentuckyoral history.org/ark:/16417/xt7qrf5kdb2t.

27. Bulvid interview, June 5, 2013.

28. Butler interview, July 11, 2013.

29. See Knowles, *Disaster Experts*, 302.

30. Freudenberg et al., *Catastrophe in the Making*, 11.

31. Freudenberg et al., *Catastrophe in the Making*, 117–18.

32. Freudenberg et al., *Catastrophe in the Making*, 116–21.

33. Joby Warrick and Michael Grunwald, "Investigators Link Levee Failures to Design Flaws," *Washington Post*, October 24, 2005, https://www.washingtonpost.com/archive/politics/2005/10/24/investigators-link-levee-failures-to-design-flaws/d6dc41b1-4c31-4040-a692-0b6ba9bfb36f/.

34. Warrick and Grunwald, "Investigators Link Levee Failures to Design Flaws."

35. Knowles, *Disaster Experts*, 295.

36. Neil M. Maher, "Introduction: Nature's Next Exit? or Why New Jersey Is as Important as Yellowstone National Park," in *New Jersey's Environments: Past, Present, and Future*, ed. Neil Maher (New Brunswick, NJ: Rutgers University Press, 2006), 2.

37. Heather Fenyk and David H. Guston, "Citizen Expertise and Citizen Action in the Creation of the Freshwater Wetlands Protection Act," in *New Jersey's Environments: Past, Present, and Future*, ed. Neil Maher (New Brunswick, NJ: Rutgers University Press, 2006), 69–70.

38. Fenyk and Guston, "Citizen Expertise and Citizen Action," 85.

39. New Jersey Department of Environmental Protection, "Blue Acres Floodplain Acquisitions," accessed July 18, 2018, https://www.nj.gov/dep/greenacres/blue_flood_ ac.html.

40. Mireya Navarro, "Christie Pulls New Jersey from 10-State Climate Initiative," *New York Times*, May 26, 2011, https://www.nytimes.com/2011/05/27/nyregion/christie-pulls-nj-from-greenhouse-gas-coalition.html.

41. This tally also includes "resilient" and "resiliency."

42. Ben Adler, "Why Is Chris Christie Silent on Climate Change, Even as New Jersey Is Threatened by Rising Seas?," *Grist*, January 9, 2014, https://grist.org/climate-energy/why-is-chris-christie-silent-on-climate-change-even-as-new-jersey-is-threatened-by-rising-seas/.

43. Erin O'Neill, "NJ's Proposed Coastal Rules Changes Spark Criticism from Environmentalists, *New Jersey Star Ledger*, June 25, 2014, https://www.nj.com/news/index.ssf/2014/06/njs_proposed_changes_to_coastal_rules.html.

44. Adler, "Why Is Chris Christie Silent on Climate Change?"

45. "Christie Administration Still Wearing Blinders on Sea Level Rise: Editorial," *New Jersey Star Ledger*, June 29, 2014, https://www.nj.com/opinion/index.ssf/2014/06/chris tie_administration_ignores_climate_change_in_rebuilding_rules_editorial.html.

46. Alexander Kaufman, "Chris Christie Leaves a Trumpian Legacy on Climate Change. But It Won't Last," *Huffington Post*, August 22, 2017, https://www.huffingtonpost.com/entry/chris-christie-climate-change_us_599c3103e4b04c532f445801.

47. Hadrien Malier, "Greening the Poor: The Trap of Moralization," *British Journal of Sociology* 70, no. 5 (2019): 1661–80; Kimin Eom et al., "Social Class, Control, and Action: Socioeconomic Status Differences in Antecedents of Support for Pro-Environmental Action," *Journal of Experimental Social Psychology* 77 (July 2018): 60–75.

48. Kailani Koenig, "Chris Christie: Climate Change a Distraction," *MSNBC.com*, May 29, 2013, http://www.msnbc.com/all-in/chris-christie-climate-change.

49. "Governor Christie: Sandy Cleanup to Cost New Jersey $29.4 Billion, *NBC New York*, November 23, 2012, https://www.nbcnewyork.com/news/local/Superstorm-Sandy-New-Jersey-Cleanup-Costs-Christie-Announcement-180644661.html.

50. "Atlantic City Resumes Tourism Advertising Post–Hurricane Sandy, Atlantic City Alliance press release, November 19, 2012, https://www.prnewswire.com/news-releases/atlantic-city-resumes-tourism-advertising-post-hurricane-sandy-179981711.html.

51. Larry Olmsted, "Post–Hurricane Sandy: Your Tourism Can Help," *Forbes*, November 1, 2012, https://www.forbes.com/sites/larryolmsted/2012/11/01/post-hurricane-sandy-your-tourism-can-help/#5b0a7cf1c5a3.

52. reNew Jersey Stronger, "New Jersey Five Years Post-Sandy: Stronger Than the Storm" (Trenton: New Jersey Department of Community Affairs, October 27, 2017), 136, 231. Copy in author's possession.

53. Butler interview, July 11, 2013.

54. Perroth interview, March 25, 2013.

55. Butler interview, July 11, 2013.

56. Perroth interview, March 25, 2013.

57. Bulvid interview, June 5, 2013.

58. Knowles, "Learning from Disaster?," 776.

59. Knowles, *Disaster Experts*, 247. Scholars have written at length about the economic and racial inequality that was exposed during Katrina.

60. Darlene Finch, phone conversation with the author, March 2, 2017. Note in author's possession.

61. Kelly interview, September 4, 2013.

62. Butler interview, July 11, 2013.

## EPILOGUE

1. Collette Kennedy, phone conversation with the author, July 2, 2018. Notes in author's possession.

2. Kennedy phone conversation, July 2, 2018.

3. Raven Rentas, "As 2020 Sunsets: A Candid Conversation with Keyport Mayor Collette J. Kennedy," *Tap Into Hazlet and Keyport*, December 31, 2020, https://www.tapinto.net/towns/hazlet-and-keyport/sections/government/articles/as-2020-sunsets-a-candid-conversation-with-keyport-mayor-collette-j-kennedy.

4. Kennedy phone conversation, July 2, 2018.

5. Kennedy phone conversation, July 2, 2018.

6. Collette Kennedy, Keyport Council Member Facebook page, May 1, 2016, https://www.facebook.com/Collette-Kennedy-Keyport-Councilmember-860742277404986/.

7. Kennedy phone conversation, July 2, 2018.

8. Kennedy phone conversation, July 2, 2018.

9. Kennedy phone conversation, July 2, 2018.

10. Mary Jane Michalak interview, October 23, 2013.

11. Dorr interview, March 22, 2013.

12. Butler interview, July 11, 2013.

13. Anthony Cavallo interview, August 20, 2013.

14. Anthony Cavallo interview, August 20, 2013.

15. United States Army Corps of Engineers, "Raritan Bay and Sandy Hook Bay, Port Monmouth, NJ Flood Risk Management Project," report, undated. Copy in author's possession; JoAnne Castagna, "Army Corps Builds Foundation for Resiliency," United States Army Corps of Engineers, July 27, 2017, https://www.nan.usace.army.mil/Media/News-Stories/Story-Article-View/Article/1259913/army-corps-builds-foundation-for-resiliency/; "Work Continues on Port Monmouth Flood Control Project," *Middletown Matters* newsletter, Spring 2018.

16. MaryAnn Spoto, "$110M Port Monmouth Flood Control Project Will Ease Storm Fears, Officials Say," *New Jersey Star Ledger*, August 1, 2014, https://www.nj.com/mon mouth/index.ssf/2014/08/110m_port_monmouth_flood_control_project_will_ease_ storm_fears_officials_say.html; Bixby interview, May 15, 2015.

17. JoAnne Castagna, "Port Monmouth Flood Control System Performing as Designed," *Atlantic Highlands Herald*, September 22, 2020, https://www.ahherald.com/ newsbrief/local-news/27560-port-monmouth-flood-control-system-performing-as-designed.

18. Miranda interview, May 15, 2013.

19. Miranda interview, May 15, 2013.

20. Charles Zusman, "Three Years in the Making, This Is One Beautiful Boat," *New Jersey Star Ledger*, October 4, 2012, updated January 18, 2019, http://blog.nj.com/boat ing/2012/10/three_years_in_the_making_this.html.

21. Zusman, "Three Years in the Making."

22. Robert Pulsch, interview by Ruqayyah Abdullah, March 19, 2015, Staring Out to Sea: Hurricane Sandy Oral History Project, Louie B. Nunn Center for Oral History, University of Kentucky Libraries, Lexington, https://kentuckyoralhistory.org/ark:/16417/ xt7mw669617v.

23. Michael Melfi interview, September 24, 2013.

24. Kelly interview, May 28, 2015.

25. Amanda Oglesby, "Governor Christie: NJ to Buy More Flood-Prone Homes," *Asbury Park Press*, October 23, 2017, https://www.app.com/story/news/local/land-envi ronment/2017/10/23/gov-christie-nj-buy-more-flood-prone-homes/790979001/.

26. Kelly interview, May 28, 2015.

27. Mary Edwards, interviewed by Ruqayyah Abdullah, March 19, 2015, Staring Out to Sea: Hurricane Sandy Oral History Project, Louie B. Nunn Center for Oral History, University of Kentucky Libraries, Lexington, https://kentuckyoralhistory.org/ark:/16417/ xt751c1thm70.

28. Gelhaus interview, September 4, 2013.

29. Kelly interview, May 28, 2015.

30. Michele S. Byer, "Blue Acres: A Win-Win for Open Space, Owners of Flooded Homes," New Jersey Conservation Foundation, August 18, 2016, reprinted on August 22, 2016, https://centraljersey.com/2016/08/22/blue-acres-is-a-win-win-for-open-space-owners-of-flooded-homes/. Copy of original in author's possession. By September 2019, the state had secured funding for 1,022 properties, had made offers on 967, and had completed its 700th closing. In total, they had demolished more than 640 homes across nine counties. Justin Auciello of National Public Radio's local affiliate, WHYY, reported, "The vast majority of the demolished homes were along inland and coastal waterways, including Ocean Township, an Ocean County municipality on the Barnegat Bay . . . and Monmouth County's Keansburg." Justin Auciello, "NJ Flood Zone Buyout Program Purchases 700th Property," *WHYY Down the Shore*, September 25, 2019, https://whyy.org/articles/n-j-flood-zone-buyout-program-purchases-700th-property/.

31. Justin Auciello, "New Jersey Infuses $75 Million into Flood Buyout Program," *WHYY Down the Shore*, October 26, 2017, https://whyy.org/articles/n-j-infuses-75-mil lion-flood-buyout-program/.

32. Nick Corasaniti, "Jersey Shore Towns Scramble for Revenue as Sandy Aid Dries Up," *New York Times*, July 30, 2017, https://www.nytimes.com/2017/07/30/nyregion/hur ricane-sandy-jersey-shore-towns.html.

33. Roger Michalak interview, October 23, 2013.

34. Butler interview, July 11, 2013.

35. Collette Kennedy, discussion with the author, May 28, 2018. Notes in author's possession.

36. Millie Gonzalez interview, June 12, 2013.
37. Kelly interview, May 28, 2015.
38. Bulvid interview, June 5, 2013.
39. Anthony Cavallo interview, August 20, 2013.
40. Anthony Cavallo interview, August 20, 2013.
41. Jeanne Cavallo, interview by Trudi-Ann Lawrence, August 20, 2013, Staring Out to Sea: Hurricane Sandy Oral History Project, Louie B. Nunn Center for Oral History, University of Kentucky Libraries, Lexington, https://kentuckyoralhistory.org/ark:/16417/xt7tqj77wv52.
42. Anthony Cavallo interview, August 20, 2013.
43. Linda Gonzalez interview, March 20, 2013.
44. Cortale interview, June 19, 2013.
45. Kelly interview, May 28, 2015.
46. Rentas, "As 2020 Sunsets."

## APPENDIX B

1. Passages from this section are drawn from an article previously published in the *Oral History Review* and from an unpublished draft article. See Abigail Perkiss, "Staring Out to Sea and the Transformative Power of Oral History for Undergraduate Interviewers," *Oral History Review* 43, no. 2 (September 2016): 392–407, copyright © 2016 The Oral History Association, reprinted by permission of Taylor & Francis Ltd, http://www.tandfonline.com on behalf of The Oral History Association; and Abigail Perkiss and Katherine Scott, "Meaningful Partnerships: Staring Out to Sea and the Role of Institutional Collaboration in Public History Work" (unpublished paper, 2015), used with permission from Scott.

2. For more on this meeting, see chapter six.

3. Mary Piasecki, speech, Port Monmouth American Legion, Port Monmouth, NJ, March 21, 2013.

4. Mary Piasecki, "Getting Their Voices Heard," Staring Out to Sea course blog, March 22, 2013, http://staringouttosea.com/.

5. In the years since we began this work 2013, oral historians have taken up the issue of oral history and trauma with new levels of intention and methodological scrutiny. In this emerging field of trauma-informed oral history, scholars and practitioners have pushed us to consider the unique methodological and theoretical challenges of this work, from preparing to interview to the process of recording, from protecting narrators to debriefing interviewers, from transcribing to processing to evaluating the stories themselves. See, for example, Mary Marshall Clark, "Case Study: Field Notes on Catastrophe; Reflections on the September 11, 2001, Oral History Memory and Narrative Project," *The Oxford Handbook of Oral History*, ed. Donald A. Ritchie (New York: Oxford University Press, 2018); Mark Cave and Stephen Sloan, eds., *Listening on the Edge: Oral History in the Aftermath of Crisis* (New York: Oxford University Press, 2014); Erin Jessee, "Managing Danger in Oral Historical Fieldwork," *Oral History Review* 44, no. 2 (2017): 322–47; "'First, Do No Harm': Tread Carefully Where Oral History, Trauma, and Current Crises Intersect," *Oral History Review* 47, no. 2 (2020), 203–13; Liz Strong, "Shifting Focus: Interviewers Share Advice on Protecting Themselves from Harm," *Oral History Review* 48, no. 2 (2021): 196–215; Kristi Girdharry, "Organizational Sponsorship: An Ethical Framework for Community Oral History Projects," *Oral History Review* 48, no. 2 (2021): 246–57. Strong's and Girdharry's articles are part of a special issue on oral history and ethics. See also "Troy Reeves on Building our Practice of Self-Care," *Oral History Review* blog, December 4, 2020, https://oralhistoryreview.org/oha-annual-meeting/troy-reeves-on-self-care/.

6. The project website is http://www.staringouttosea.com. Student reflections on the course and the process of developing the project are available there.

7. Arij Syed, "Preparing for the Interview Process," Staring Out to Sea course blog, March 5, 2013, http://staringouttosea.com/.

8. One of the more noteworthy insights to come out of these original interviews was the need to ask directly about the narrator's race. We knew we wanted to look at socio-economic indicators in evaluating storm response, but not until the students began their interviews did we realize that the audio format would be limiting unless we added specific questions about identity politics.

9. Brittany Le Strange, class reflection, May 2013. Document in author's possession.

10. StoryCorps launched in 2003 from radio producer David Isay. The initiative creates accessible spaces for conducting and recording short interviews between two people who have a relationship with each other. As of 2020, StoryCorps has recorded more than sixty thousand interviews. They are archived at the American Folklife Center at the Library of Congress.

11. Jennifer Reut, "Oral History Projects Document Hurricane Sandy," *Perspectives on History*, October 2013, 10–11.

# Index

CPSIA information can be obtained
at www.ICGtesting.com
Printed in the USA
LVHW032040300323
743031LV00003B/494